Ashford Castle

Through the centuries

Cadogan Publications Limited
1-3 Dungar Terrace, Dun Laoghaire, Dublin
Tel: ++353 1 2300322   Fax: ++353 1 2300629

7 Verney House, 1B Hollywood Road, London SW10 9HS, UK
Tel: 44-20-77 95 01 82   Fax: 44-20-77 95 09 25

27 West 24th Street, Suite 302, New York, NY 10010, USA
Tel: 1-212-414 8776   Fax: 1-212-414 8779

British Library Cataloguing in Publication Data
A catalogue record for this book is available from The British Library
ISBN 0-9534276-3-3

Publisher: **Kevin Kelly**
Group Editorial Director: **Sonya Perkins**
Art Director: **John Rook**

Colour origination by Typeform Repro
Printed by Artes Graficas Toledo, Spain
DLTO: 1645-2000

Ashford Castle

Through the centuries

by Olda FitzGerald
Photography by Mike Bunn

Historical photographs provided by
David Davison

CP

Contents

Acknowledgements

I have learnt so much while writing this book and the only reason that I have been able to finish it has been due to the generous support given to me by all those who knew about the subject and were prepared to share their knowledge.

First and foremost I must thank my husband Desmond, whose library at Glin Castle has been my constant resource and whose help and research on my behalf has been invaluable. My thanks also to my publisher Kevin Kelly, his very supportive editorial director Sonya Perkins, and his art director, John Rook. The late Maurice Semple and all his works were my beacon in the early darkness. Simon and Alice Boyd and Charlotte Mitchell were able to point me in the right direction early on, and Miranda Iveagh gave me valuable advice. Charles Plunket was extremely helpful and went to great lengths to find me what I needed. Desmond Guinness shared his family memories and Anthony Malcomson responded immediately and succinctly to my cry for recondite information. Charles Nelson's knowledge of Irish garden history and his kindness in sharing this knowledge has been of great assistance. William Everett was a valuable and hospitable link in the chain of discovery, and my thanks are due to the Archivist of the Guinness Ireland Archives at St. James' Gate. They are also due to David Griffin and the staff of the Irish Architectural Archive, and to the Librarian at the National Botanic Gardens, Glasnevin, who gave me every assistance possible as did the Librarian at Trinity College Library. Sinead MacCoole provided me with difficult to source information at breakneck speed, and Bernard Williams kindly lent me *A Lay of Ashford*. Patrick Melvin went to endless trouble and Kevin B. Nowlan read the text and offered valuable suggestions. Valerie Pakenham gave me good advice, and Michael Gibbons and Kathleen Villiers-Tuthill were generous with their help. Dom Oranmore and Browne talked about his family history and his memories of life at Ashford Castle casting a sharp and amused eye on things I might otherwise have missed. His son Garech Browne was enormously helpful and enthusiastic, lending me books, and introducing me to the historian Randal MacDonnell whose researches were invaluable. Sheila Wilson Wright told me about her County Mayo childhood, and Bridget Clesham was most helpful. Arthur Shackleton guided me with his garden research and Patrick Bowe, Terence Reeves Smyth and Nicola Gordon-Bowe all gave me the benefit of their knowledge.

Above all I am grateful to Kevin Crowe, the Chairman of the Board of Directors of Ashford Castle for his support, and to Sheila O'Malley who brought the idea for this book to me, and saw me through the process. To manager Rory Murphy and his staff who made my stays at Ashford Castle so comfortable and were so thoughtful and helpful in every way. Particular thanks to Michael Duggan and Paula Carroll for smoothing my path and providing vital assistance. So much information was provided by historian and forester Peter Campbell who with executive chef Denis Lenihan and head fishing ghillie Frank Costello built up a picture for me of real life at Ashford Castle both in the past and today. Mike Bunn the brilliant photographer was able to catch the weather and produce these ravishing and evocative photographs, and David Davison reproduced the images from the past with crystal clarity.

On the home front I must thank my mother Georgina Willes for putting up with my continual distraction, and my children Catherine, Nesta, and Honor for helping me in every way. My thanks to Bob Duff for running Glin Castle so smoothly, to Seamus Hogan for his superb cooking, to Thomas Wall for improving the garden while I typed, and to Martin Foley, Mary Foley, and Larry Power, for their support. My thanks to Mary Reade and Evelyn O'Sullivan who have done so much over the years to help us keep the show on the road.

Olda FitzGerald

Foreword

I could see a view across a Lough to mountains beyond, and in the middle of the scene stood a building, around which stretched hills and woods and fields and walls into infinity. But what was I looking at? I stretched out a tentative hand to touch the rough stone wall of the De Burgos original tower in Ashford Castle and in that instant I determined to find an explanation. It has been a voyage of discovery and I have felt as though I was peeling away the many skins of an onion to reach the perfect centre. How had this vast building come to be here, how to explain the different styles of building, and not only that, but how had it become a successful hotel? Who had planted the gardens and woods? What did it all represent and who were the people who built it? How had it affected people's lives and who had lived here and how did it work today? This was what I set out to discover that autumn afternoon in 1999. All these questions came crowding into my head and for a weak moment I felt that it would be quite impossible to ever grasp such a conundrum.

It has been similar to finding lost pieces of a jigsaw puzzle and I hope that as you turn the pages you will accompany me on my search. Step by step the picture became clearer as I burrowed further and further into books and manuscripts, peered at maps, and gazed at prints, drawings, and early photographs. Gradually the outline of the characters appeared, and as they did so, the outline of the buildings became clearer as well. I started to feel more confident as the whole history of an area was unrolled before me, and the mist in front of my eyes began to melt away.

In researching the lives of Lord and Lady Ardilaun it has been difficult to have had no actual voices to listen to, except in their formal letters written to newspapers or reports from friends in journals. The Ardilauns were two of the greatest philanthropists of their day, and yet very little has been written about them and very few of their letters have been published. I have caught glimpses of them here and there, but they still remain the distant, cool, gracious couple of their photographs rather than living breathing human beings. A blank wall is a frustrating obstacle in any search and always leads one to wonder whether there is anything curious behind it. Many pieces of the jigsaw are still missing, but my hope is that by reading these chapters, researchers will be encouraged to delve deeper. Perhaps when the Bantry archives and the Farmleigh Iveagh papers have been re-catalogued more information will be available. Indeed, Nigel Everett has been working on the Bantry archives and in his new book *Wild Gardens* his summation of the marriage is based on his discoveries there: 'She was happy to accept what was always understood to be a purely platonic marriage in exchange for an unusual degree of personal and material independence … Guinness was keen to disguise his unconventional life.'

The evolution of Ashford Castle has been a fascinating trail and I hope that my readers will share with me the mounting excitement I felt as the West of Ireland in all its wistful beauty was revealed before me.

Olda FitzGerald

The Owners of Ashford Castle

c.1228: The de Burgos lay the first stone

↓

1855: Col. Dominick Browne of Castle Mc Garrett and Ashford,
grandfather of Dominick, 1st Baron Oranmore and Browne,
sold Ashford

↓

1855: Sir Benjamin Lee Guinness and Elizabeth (Bessie) Guinness
bought Ashford

↓

1868: Sir Arthur Edward Guinness, 1st Lord Ardilaun, married
Lady Olive White, and inherited Ashford from his father

↓

1915: Sir Edward Cecil Guinness, 1st Earl of Iveagh, married Adelaide
Guinness, his cousin, and inherited Ashford from his brother

↓

1939: The Hon. Ernest Guinness married Mairie Clotilde Russell,
inherited the estate from his father in 1927,
and sold it to the Irish State

↓

1939–1969: Castle leased to Noel Huggard and run as an hotel

↓

1969: Castle bought by John A Mulcahy

↓

1985: Castle bought by Consortium

A Bird's Eye View

*T*he roads leading through the ancient undulating landscape of the West of Ireland to Ashford Castle snake through a patchwork quilt of different greens. Woolly sheep seem to be woven into the pattern of the County Galway fields divided by little stone walls from the gleaming blue waters of Lough Corrib. A majestic stand of trees and a baronial cut stone gateway announce our arrival and we whirl past the golf course and down towards the castle.

Standing transfixed by the cut stone machiolations, turrets, towers, arrow loops, cremlins and merlins and all the ferocious accoutrements of the high Victorian's idea of the 'true rust' of the Baron's wars, it is just possible to glimpse in the core of this astonishing building the original castle of the Norman family, the de Burgos—later the Burkes—who laid the first stone around 1228. Silhouetted dramatically between the waters of Lough Corrib and the County Mayo sky—the Counties of Galway and Mayo dexterously changing feet on the bridge that crosses the moat—the castle today, though much enlarged, still seems to dominate the landscape with the same single-minded assurance of 800 years ago.

Originally the de Burgos would have watched for their enemy's approach across the Lough from a bleak stone tower, with a redout built up against the water. Since then that tower has been incorporated into the most luxurious, stately, and comfortable hotel in the whole of Ireland. There are 83 ensuite bedrooms, two vast dining-rooms, halls, a minstrel's gallery, drawing-rooms, the Prince of Wales bar—to commemorate the visit in 1905 of the future English monarch King George V—and a large and

invariably welcoming and professional staff. Exquisite food is produced by a culinary team under Head Chef Denis Lenihan in the suite of kitchens and, under the 26-year captainship of Manager Rory Murphy, this great hotel steams confidently ahead into the future. Rows and rows of official testimonials record the consistently high quality of food, service, and comfort. Photographs of appreciative celebrities who have stayed here over the years line the walls and, although the castle has been a hotel since 1939, the highest standards of entertaining have always prevailed, even when the castle was in private hands.

From the proud Norman de Burgos in the 13th century, who built the original tower, the property passed to the Norman family of de Brun. The de Bruns later changed their name to Browne and, later still, were created Barons Oranmore and Browne in 1836. Their 'Ashford House' which they built further along from the tower facing the Lough, boasted a high roof in the style of a small French chateau centred with their heraldic stone two-headed eagle. This building was incorporated by Lord Ardilaun into his 1860s castle.

Like many other landlords the Oranmore and Brownes were nearly bankrupted after the famine and the estate was sold in 1855 through the Encumbered Estates Court to Sir Benjamin Lee Guinness 1st. Baronet, of the great Guinness brewing dynasty. The property passed, on Sir Benjamin's death in 1868, to his eldest son Sir Arthur Guinness, later Lord Ardilaun who married in 1871 Lady Olivia White, daughter of the 3rd Earl of Bantry of Bantry House, County Cork. Lady Ardilaun was a keen gardener and both she and her devoted husband enlarged and adorned the castle and gardens during their lifetime. They were tremendous philanthropists, but had no children so after Lord Ardilaun's death in 1915 Ashford Castle was left to his brother the 1st Earl of Iveagh.

Lord Iveagh lived until 1927 and was the competent, philanthropic and very active head of the Brewery. The estate passed after his death through the Iveagh trustees to his third son, the Hon. Ernest Guinness who finally sold the 22,000 acre estate to the Irish State for £20,000 on 30 April 1939. Far from being abandoned and falling into ruinous decay, as has been the fate of so many great houses in Ireland, this was to be the fruitful beginnings of the castle's new life as a great hotel and a continuance of the hospitable tradition under which it had flourished over the centuries.

Following the purchase, the Irish State handed over all the arable lands to the Land Commission, which divided it into parcels and gave them to the local farmers, and the Department of Forestry took over the acreage that was planted with trees. One hundred and fifty acres were allocated to the castle as a separate unit and was leased for 45 years at a nominal rent by hotelier Noel Huggard, whose family owned the Butler Arms at Waterville in County Kerry.

Retired forester Peter Campbell remembers how this came about, when two of the men who worked with the Forestry Department—Owen Mooney and Sean O'Sullivan—were being sent on a forestry course to

Above, Little has changed since musicians played in the gallery of the hall for Lady Ardilaun's dancers in Victorian and Edwardian days
Left, The entrance gate lodge

Germany. As they travelled there they met a man at Euston Station in London with whom they had been at school at Clongowes, the great Irish public school near Dublin. That man was Noel Huggard. When he heard from his old friends that Ashford Castle—which had never been anything but a private home—was for rent—he immediately had the idea of turning it into a hotel. The fate of the building, and of all those who worked in it, was thus decided by an extraordinarily coincidental meeting!

During World War II Noel Huggard developed the hotel so that it especially catered for guests who wanted to fish. This was an obvious move, as some of the best brown trout fishing in Europe was found in Lough Corrib. British

Army officers on leave from the battlefronts of Europe, flocked to Ashford to escape the privations of wartime food rationing in England. Cream, butter, milk, fish, meat, and whiskey were all plentiful and the hotel started to hum. There were two hackney cabs in the area that began to ferry guests to and from the railway station. The number of visitors increased, and what might have been a liability became an asset. After the War the officers returned with their wives and girlfriends and under Noel Huggard's personal management the hotel moved into the top rank of Irish hotels of the day.

When Noel Huggard finally retired down to his family-run inn in County Kerry in 1970, the hotel was

The Great Hall

*Heraldic pomp in stone—
Lord Ardilaun's coat of
arms on the Castle walls*

bought by John A. Mulcahy, a successful Irishman from
Wexford who had made a fortune in the US. When
Pat Nixon visited Ireland to research her roots, Mulcahy,
who was a great friend of the President, was on hand
to help her. They lunched at Ashford Castle and Mulcahy
fell in love with the place. He returned for a second
visit that same year and then bought the hotel in 1971.
Once again, coincidence played a part in the fate of
the castle.

Much of Mulcahy's time in the late 1960s and early
1970s was devoted to promoting Ireland and encouraging
American industrialists to invest in the country. Manager
Rory Murphy recalls: 'He would lease a 707 jet, fly in

American businessmen, and, wining and dining them, guide them around the country on a seven-day tour. He would then give each of them a present of a picture of the West of Ireland painted by his friend the artist Frank Egginton, and say "Thank you for coming to my country. Now what are you going to do about it?." A lot of them didn't come back, but some, such as Pfizer Pharmaceuticals did!'

John Mulcahy arranged to buy the castle in 1971, and had a vision of a larger hotel with superb American plumbing and a bigger inner dining room. He developed the building, adding 40 more bedrooms and en-suite bathrooms that took advantage of the extraordinary views over the water. It took three years to build the new wing and the golf course and Mulcahy invested £1.5 million in the re-invigoration of the hotel. When the locals, who were very impressed by this, heard Mulcahy was going to build a swimming pool they remarked that it was more likely that he was going to heat the Corrib instead!

Mulcahy retired in 1984 and sold the hotel to the present consortium, a group of well-known Irish and American investors. They purchased one of the most splendid hotels in the country, with a growing international reputation that is increasing every year. As well as the superbly run hotel there are 500 acres of gardens and park and five of the 365 islands on the Corrib. The facilities include an equestrian centre, the first falconry school in Ireland, tennis courts, two large fishing boats, archery and clay pigeon shooting facilities.

Every year, Captain Mark Phillips—the first husband of the Princess Royal of England—directs a pre-hunting course at the Equestrian Centre. He comfortably initiates the rider into the mysteries of fox-hunting in the West of Ireland, giving the visitor the confidence to get to know their horse and take off on their own on the great day.

The story of the building and the estate down through the centuries involves gathering together all the different historical threads and weaving them into a great tapestry. There are the lives of the people who lived here and their place in the society of their time; there is the topography of the landscape and the story of the planting of the gardens together with the myths, legends, and traditions that are associated with every scrap of land or lump of stone; there is the archeological shape of the lakeside; there is the initial building and the rebuilding of the castle; there is also the relationship of the local community with the owners; there are the vivid local recollections of some of the most formative events in the nation's history seen through the myths, mists, and genealogical contortions of the past.

Each owner briefly takes centre stage against the background of Lough Corrib in an effort to make the stage-set match his aspirations, only to vanish and be seen no more. To understand the story of the estate we must make the journey from the lonely tower house of the Normans in the 12th century to the many towered castle of the 21st century that sits proudly on Lough Corrib amidst the wild beauty of the West of Ireland.

Fully caparisoned men-at-arms should be riding across the bridge designed by George Ashlin. Lord Ardilaun's coronet and initials decorate the battlements of the gatehouse

The First Threads of the Tapestry

*T*he bewitching view over Lough Corrib, according to local archaeologist Michael Gibbons, has not changed since the days when nomadic Mesolithic hunter-gatherers trapped the fish and hunted the fowl and wild boar that lived on the shores of the Lough.

Six thousand years ago these early Irishmen left behind them their implements in a midden of oyster, limpet, and periwinkle shells that have been recently discovered in a turlough—a small lake that periodically dries up and then appears again—in the nearby village of Cong. The stunning prehistoric sights around the village and locality include the Neolithic tomb in Tobermiroge, which would have been used as a communal burial ground and is a testament to the early thriving farming people that cleared the ancient forests of Cong. The ten-metre high Ballymacgibbon Cairn near the village of Cross is one of the largest prehistoric cairns in the country and in all probability contains the remains of a large Passage Tomb. The most beautiful of all the prehistoric sites are the group of four Stone Circles at *Moyatura Cunga* (Plain of the Pillar) built in the Bronze Age and considered by the 19th century scholar Sir William Wilde (father of Oscar, who had a lodge near Cong which he called Moytura) to have been Druidic temples. These are also sometimes thought to have been primitive astronomical observatories. The spectacularly sited Eochy's hilltop cairn where white stone after white stone has been built up to an enormous height would have been a place of tribal gatherings and possibly an inauguration centre in pre-Christian times. Further evidence of Bronze Age settlement is the recently excavated cooking site *Fulachta Fiadha* at Ballinrobe.

Below, A bearded caryatid from a 17th century doorway to a Galway city merchant's house now guards the entrance to the sunken garden
Opposite, Entrance to the coffee house on Inchigoill Island

In the Celtic Iron Age 1500–2500 years ago, massive fortifications were being constructed by warrior elites all around the country and the banks of the great lakes were dotted with lakeforts such as Hag's Castle on Lough Mask, one of the largest in the country. Smaller forts often had underground chambers or souterrains — in prehistoric times the vast mineral wealth of Connemara and Mayo would have been channelled across the narrows of Cong and into the more fertile and populated regions of the interior. The groupings of burial and ritual monuments suggest that a highly evolved social elite was growing rich, not just on the fruits of the land, but on a valuable trade in gold from Croagh Patrick, soapstone from the islands of Inishbofin and Inishark, and marble from Connemara. Cong was a gateway to Connemara and a crossroads for the north/south trade to the Mayo interior via the great chain of the lakes Corrib, Mask and Carra.

Folklore and the *Annals of the Four Masters* claim that here on this ancient plain among these relics of pagan times was fought the great battle of Moytura between the rival peoples of the Firbolg and the de Daanan. Much of the evidence—such as pagan temples, altars, pillar stones inscribed with Ogham writing, great cromlechs, and tumuli built with stone—was destroyed in later times to provide building stones and gate posts for farmers or demolished in the excavation of sand pits. Eochy's cairn, standing 60 foot high and once surrounded by great standing stones overlooking the Mask and Corrib and the whole western panorama from Nephin to the Twelve Pins, is alleged to have been the burial mound of King Eochy, the last of the Firbolg kings of Ireland who fell at the battle of Moytura more than 3,000 years ago. The scholar and eye-surgeon to Queen Victoria, Sir William Wilde, believed this to be the case. He wrote an identifying description of the ground-plan of the battle and found a sepulchre urn in a nearby cave in 1886 which he gave to the Royal Hibernian Academy in Dublin for safe-keeping.

The Tuatha de Dannan were said to be handsome, well dressed, musical, intellectual, magnanimous, determined, fearless, skilled in magic, arts and crafts. When their king, Nuada, lost his hand in battle they made him a silver hand as a replacement. The Firbolgs on the other hand were small and dark, with distended stomachs from eating clay, and skilled in shipbuilding and navigation. A furious conflict ensued with great valour displayed on both sides. Shields were smashed, spears shivered, swords broken, hand-to-hand encounters took place, youth and veteran were slaughtered and cairns erected. So many heroes including the king of the Firbolgs had been killed after four days of fighting that the two sides met and decided to make peace and divide the country between them. Druids, bards, and poets celebrated the battle and the mythology is vividly detailed and precise, with the Plain of Moytura being claimed as the exact site of the contest that took place 3,000 years ago.

The Irish name for Cong is *Cunga* a word that was used in Old Irish to describe a narrow neck of land between two sheets of water. And Cong indeed stands between

Loughs Mask and Corrib. In 623 on a little oasis among the limestone rocks St. Fechin founded a church, a small oratory surrounded by beehive-shaped dwelling-huts made of mud and wattle. Cong has been known in Irish ever since then as *Cunga Feicin* (Feichin's Neck of Land between the Waters); a perfect description of invisible rushing underground rivers that filter the water through the limestone from Lough Mask to Lough Corrib under the village and surrounding landscape of Cong. The waters flow through limitless caves and underground caverns, then rise to the surface shining and almost boiling at 'The Meeting of the Waters' in Cong before plunging with a swallowing gurgle, back down into the earth through the slugga or swallow holes in the rock to emerge later in Lough Corrib. The entire limestone plateau is a maze of underground channels, and the many caves are actually shafts running down to a long underground water tunnel. Sometimes the underground rumblings become so loud

The cloisters at Cong Abbey, which were restored by Sir Benjamin Lee Guinness

that in certain places they used be explained away as 'the little people' grinding their corn for the winter in 'the Leprechaun's Mill'. The water rises again at various colourfully named spots such as 'the Round Hill of the Oozing Water', 'the Footstep of the Hag' and 'the Waterhole of the Young Fairies'. Even the caves themselves are the subject of historic tradition and fairy stories.

'Webb's Cave' is named after Captain FitzGerald Webb—a person of great influence in Connaught and, it was said, as gentlemanly a man as ever drove a ball through another's lungs—who was the 18th century Bluebeard of the West. Webb seduced and then murdered nine girls by luring them to his den, having his way with them, and then hurling them down into the hole in the cave and leaving them to drown. The tenth girl was, however, more wily than the rest, and managed to push her seducer into the hole instead. 'Kelly's Cave' was named after a highwayman whose family had been driven from

land that had been theirs for countless generations. 'The Pigeon Hole' is so called because of the clouds of pigeons that used to emerge from it. According to the old story-tellers, when a beautiful girl's lover, the Squire's son, was drowned in the lake, she became demented with grief. The fairies took pity on her and turned her into a little trout that swims safely in the pool in the cave waiting for her true love to join her. One day a soldier caught the trout, cutting its side slightly with a knife, and was about to put it in a pan for his dinner when he was suddenly confronted by a furious lovely young girl with a cut on her arm who demanded to be put back into the pool immediately. Turning round in surprise he saw instead a little trout lying on the floor of the cave, which he hastily dropped back into the water. Ever since, or so the story goes, all the local trout have a red mark on their sides from the cut inflicted by the soldier.

> *'Ye Pigeon Hole of story fame,*
> *Ungallant was that soldier*
> *Who tried to fry a noble dame*
> *He brought from regions colder!'*

Lough Corrib is said to be named after the celebrated navigator of the Tuatha de Danann, one of whose names was *Mannanan Mac Lir* (the son of the Sea) and another was *Orbsen Mac Alloid*. This name in English sounded like Corribsen and was amended to Corrib. Orbsen Mac Alloid was a king of Ireland and a grandson of the de Danann king Nuada of the Silver Hand. The Irish speaking *shanachies* (storytellers), who lived on the shores of the Lough, had many a story to weave around his heroic exploits and genealogy.

Of the 365 islands on the Lough the most interesting is *Inchigoill (*the Island of the Devout Stranger) where St. Patrick's nephew lived and died, and built a tiny church. The Hiberno-Romanesque doorway (added in the early 12th century) is still standing. The fishing is excellent and today's boating visitors stop there so that the fishing ghillies can build a fire to cook the trout *al fresco*, and eat picnics after their arduous labours! On this little island stand the ruins of two ancient churches. There is also a graveyard and what is regarded as the oldest Christian monument in Europe, as well as the grave of the Archbishop of Tuam, Archbishop O'Nioc, who died in 1128. The ancient memorial to the Saintly Stranger is a pillar stone with a perpendicular inscription in archaic characters known as *Lie Luguaedon*, a monument to St. Patrick's nephew and fellow missionary in the west of Ireland. The inscription in Latin on the pillarstone makes it clear that we are looking at the memorial to Lugna. He was not only the son of St. Patrick's sister Limanin, but he was also, it is said in the

Above left, The stone of Luguaedon near the doorway of St. Patrick's Church on Inchigoill Island
Left, An Expansional cross with Greek fretwork patterns is incorporated within a wall of Templenaneeve Church on Inchigoill Island

ancient Book of Lecan, the Saint's navigator. Ever since surnames came into use in Ireland under the reign of Brian Boru, according to Stephen Gwynn author of *The Fair Hills of Ireland* there has been someone living on Inchigoill with an Irish name that means 'of the Saint's family'. Sadly, since the death of the last inhabitant Tom Nevin (Nevin can mean the little Saint or Saintling) this island is finally, after so many years, deserted.

The historian Donnchadh Ó Corráin tells us that monasticism made rapid strides in the early Irish church of the 6th century. These great self-governing monastic churches, each with their own rule, organisation, and estates, became in time the bearers of a rich and varied literary and artistic culture, and provided the patronage and the economic support necessary for the cultivation of high art. The churchmen brought with them to Ireland much of the learning of late antiquity, and the Irish schools of the late 6th and 7th centuries achieved a high level of scholarship. The scholars, poets and lawyers associated with the church formed a single caste and began the slow process of formulating the Law, both church and secular. In the arts generally, and above all in metalwork, illumination and calligraphy, the 7th, 8th and 9th centuries in Ireland were periods of great creativity.

The dynamic Turlough O'Connor, king of Connaught (1106–1156) was the greatest Irish warrior king of the 12th century. He built a ring of fortresses around Connaught and strategic bridges across the river Shannon, and maintained a large army and navy. O'Connor built the Royal Abbey of Cong for the Order of St. Augustine in 1120 and soon after that, in 1123, commissioned the processional Cross of Cong—the Yellow Crozier, as it was known to the people. This is one of the great glories of Irish ecclesiastical craftsmanship and is now one of the principal treasures in the National Museum in Dublin. The cross of black oak is encased in gold and silver and studded with jewels. Punched into the silver plate on its sides are a series of inscriptions in Irish that bid us pray for Turloch O Connor, King of Ireland, for whom the shrine was made, and for Murtagh O'Duffy who was the Archbishop of Connaught and for the Irish artist who made the cross. It was originally made to enshrine a fragment of the True Cross, which had been sent to King Turlough Mor O'Connor from Rome and was preserved under a large central crystal, but this has since disappeared.

Other reliquaries connected with the Abbey of Cong that can be seen in the National Museum are the Bell of St. Patrick and the Shrine of St. Patrick's Tooth, (the *Cathach*), which is a heavy gilt and silver-lidded bejewelled box that was carried into battle by the O'Donnells to bring them victory over their enemies:

> 'Here he swore upon the "cathach",
> Held aloft the willow wand,
> While ten thousand tribesmen hailed him
> And awaited his command.'

Dr. Francoise Henry gives us an idea of the interiors of early Irish churches:

Left and above, Monastic ruins of Templenaneeve Church on Inchigoill Island restored by Sir Benjamin Lee Guinness

'Chalices and bookcovers on the altar glittered with silver and gold ornament; everywhere shone the crisp gilding and studs on crosiers, shrines and censers. The lamps were resplendent with multicoloured enamels. On the vestments of the priests and probably on the cloaks of the laity, penannular brooches sparkled in the light. Seldom has the art of the goldsmith and the bronzer attained such dazzling brilliance and such technical virtuosity.'

Such descriptions help us to imagine the interiors of the Royal Abbey of Cong when the royal family of O'Connor were the patrons of the monks and the members of the royal families including King Ruari O'Connor retired to live there in their old age. The monasteries at the time were well integrated into the upper ranks of society, ruled mostly by aristocrats and the rich and politically influential, and they were important centres of economic activity. Some of the great monastic centres were the regular residences of the kings because it was these kings of provinces who exercised real power, and the annals are full of their battles and dynastic struggles to become the High King of all Ireland. *Agallamh na Senorach*, the most important literary text of the 12th century, describes a chivalrous world filled with brave young lords, fair ladies, fine clothes, feasting, adventures, beauty, honour and fidelity. However, the bloody realities of 12th century political life were quite different and, unless they had powerful defenders, life for many ordinary people was nasty, brutish and brief. The churchmen developed the idea of the ordained and consecrated king and expected in return to profit from their protection.

During times of peace, students from all over England and Europe came to study in the great monastic school at Cong, and Ireland became known as 'the Island of Saints and Scholars'. The little stone-built Monk's Fishing House still stands in the Cong river today.

The monks attached a bell to the fishing line that would ring in the Abbey when a fish took the bait, leaving the monks plenty of time to prepare their vegetables before he was ready to be cooked. The site on which Ashford Castle stands today would have been part of the Abbey property and in Irish was called *Cappacoroge* which translates as: 'the Market Garden of the Beehives'—when the Abbey was flourishing perhaps the fragrant garden overlooking the Corrib was run by

bee-keeping Brothers. Sixty years before Henry II of England arrived with all the military might and civilisation of the Normans, a native Irish king had founded an Irish Abbey and established at Cong a great school of learning that in time educated no fewer than 3,000 students and scholars.

The monastic annals record the deaths of Abbots and the appointment of their successors. They also mention great works of learning and examples of Christian charity, raids and burnings, and finally the reconstruction of the now Gothic Abbey in 1205 by Cathal O'Connor of the Wine Red Hand. He was the illegitimate son of King Turloch Mor O'Connor, and it is the ruins of his building that we see today.

St. Colmcille was of the Royal family of O'Donnell who were for a long time the owners of Cong and Cong Abbey. The Abbey was the last resting place of some of Ireland's most ambitious and distinguished early churchmen, soldiers, and intriguers as well as King Ruari O'Connor (remains were later moved to Clonmacnoise) and his daughter the Queen of Ulster — O'Connor was the king who in an attempt to subdue his unruly subjects with his ally king Dermot MacMurrough, has been cursed in Ireland ever since for inviting over the English King Henry II and his Norman knights. In doing so they changed the course of Irish history.

Below, One of the many islands in the Corrib Right, Detail from the stained glass windows of the Catholic Church in Cong by the great Irish stained glass artist, Harry Clarke

I ṪCUIṀNE ·ḊIL· AR· AN· ṪCEAṄṖORT
Miċeál O Briain
A· FUAIR· BÁr· I· DTUAr· Mic· Éadaiġ
· AN· 3ᴬᴰ · Bealtaine· 1921· R·I·P·

Chapter 3

Ghosts of the Past

T he lonely Norman towerhouse overlooking Lough Corrib has been the inspiration and foundation for all subsequent building and is now incorporated into Ashford Castle in a seamless join. In the 1860s Lord Ardilaun completely renewed the interior and the curling wooden banistered staircase winding to the top floor. From the bedrooms today there is an extraordinary view across the water to the little tufted islands on the one side and across to the shining rushing Cong river on the other.

In spite of the seamless join, you nevertheless get a little shiver from the past as you climb the stairs. These towers were built as defensive fortresses in a time of unparalleled ferocity between invaders and invaded. No mercy was shown and buildings were ruthlessly sacked, women and children instantly put to the sword, hostages murdered, revenge taken, and promises broken. The Normans, who had come to Ireland at the invitation of King Dermot MacMurrough and his ally king Ruari O'Connor, had extended their influence across the country. Several members of the powerful de Burgo family had acquired land in Galway and Mayo—this family, descended from Charlemagne, have been called at various times de Burghs, de Burgo, and in later days Burke, and Bourke. Robert de Burgh accompanied William the Conqueror from Normandy to the Battle of Hastings in 1066 and his descendant, William de Burgh founded one of the noblest and most illustrious families in Ireland. In the mid-14th century the Connaught Burkes were Hibernicised—more Irish than the Irish themselves—and adopted Gaelic dress, Brehon laws, and the language and customs of the native Irish. The Norman tower, however,

would have been built in 1228 when these proud prickly knights from the marches of Wales were still very much on the defensive. The Norman organisation in battle was second to none and the native Irish kings were hard pressed to compete with their coats of chain mail, cavalry charges, and deadly archers. This tower would have been built by the de Burgos as a defence and as a look-out across the Lough. The de Burgos were the most persevering and finally triumphant enemy of the O'Connors, whose power in Connaught they effectively destroyed. After ceaseless warfare the family firmly established their own power base, owing only a nominal allegiance to the English Crown.

Meanwhile William de Burgh was quickly becoming settled in the nearby town of Galway, where he founded a town enclosed within walls of the traditional Norman type. The disaffected and rebellious O'Flahertys were the natural enemies of the Galway merchants who, it is said, had the legend *From the ferocious O'Flahertys, O Lord deliver us* carved over one of the town gates.

The trading prowess of Galway and its' port owes its' fame to the achievements of fourteen families, mainly of Norman origin, who settled there during the 13th and 14th centuries and were known as The Tribes of Galway. The roll call of the families that are still proud today to be so named is Athy, Blake, Bodkin, Browne, Deane, Darcy, Font, French, Joyce, Kirwan, Lynch, Martin, Morris, and Skerett. The Kirwans and the Athys had been associated with the town from its earliest days before the advent of the de Burghs. Most of the other families, however, had gravitated to Galway in the train of the Norman conqueror. So it is clear that the Tribes of Galway were initially aristocratic conquistadors and then merchants in the town of Galway. When they had made their fortunes they later became landed gentry, buying property and building houses all over Counties Galway and Mayo. They never allowed anyone to forget their noble antecedents, even when they had exchanged the sword for the pen and turned to commerce. They made for themselves a powerful oligarchy in the town so that from the first, Galway was an essentially aristocratic place. The first ships to use the port were quite small and could enter the mouth of the river Corrib easily and, as there was no quay, they would beach on the slope where the Fish Market now stands.

The market in the town was one of the few places outside of Cork, Dublin and Waterford where hides and wool were allowed to be sold. The merchants of the town were quite capable of protecting their own interests and in alliance with the de Burgos agreed to pay the O'Briens of Aran a tribute of wine to ensure the safe passage of Galway ships using the bay. The inland and foreign trade grew and in 1397 King Richard II granted the town a second charter, which curtailed the power of the de Burgos and converted Galway into a Royal borough.

The fountain, blown into a thousand light-reflecting drops, looks across to some of the best brown trout fishing in Ireland

A 17th century Galway town house entrance leads into the sunken garden

In the 15th century a quay was built on the river and the commerce of the port extended into many parts of Europe and English, Scottish, French, Portuguese and Spanish ships regularly sailed into the port. The town was almost completely destroyed by fire in 1473 and, when it was rebuilt, the merchants decided to assert their independence of both the Irish Archdiocese of Tuam and the de Burgo family. The merchants appealed to their temporal and spiritual leaders, the English king and the Pope. In 1484 King Richard III granted the inhabitants a new charter that allowed them to elect a Mayor and bailiffs and finally deprived the de Burgo family of all rule and authority within Galway.

In the early days of the Norman settlement one of the de Burgo's most valiant companions in arms was Sir David le Brun, a Norman knight. He helped de Burgo conquer Connaught, for which he was granted extensive lands in Mayo and Galway where he built the castle of Carrabrowne at Oranmore, near Galway town. The castle still stands and is lived in by Leonie Leslie and her husband, the well-known traditional musician, Alec Finn. It was restored in the 1930s by her mother (the author Anita Leslie) and father, and the sailor Commander Bill King. Their Norman tower still withstands the blasts from Galway Bay and with a huge crackling fire in the original fireplace, an ox roasting, and traditional Irish pipes playing, it is not hard to imagine the pleasanter aspects of the life that was lived in these towers in medieval times. Sir David le Brun married an Irish beauty, Bevann O'Flahertie, daughter of chieftain Morragh O'Flahertie of West Connaught. They and their descendants owned huge tracts of land that were taken away from them in the confiscation which followed the Elizabethan and Cromwellian wars. le Brun's son Stephen married Catherine Bermingham, daughter of Lord Athenry, and their grandson accompanied the Earl of Kildare to the French wars in the reign of Edward III.

Colonel Dominick Browne was Mayor of Galway in 1575 and played a leading part in the affairs of the time. He was a party to 'the Galway Compositions' entered into in 1585 between Sir John Perrot and the chieftains and freeholders of Galway. Most of the landowning Brownes in County Galway were descended from one or other of Colonel Dominick's seven sons. Another Colonel Browne was again Mayor in 1688 and 1689 and commanded an infantry regiment in the Irish army of James II. The family were committed Catholics and Jacobites — the Colonel

Sir Benjamin Lee Guinness restored the lakeside redout
originally built by the de Burgos

Chapter 3

fought at the battle of Aughrim and was one of the hostages when Galway surrendered to General Ginkel in 1691.

Throughout this time the family was heavily involved in trade. In 1627 Martin Browne chartered a boat at La Rochelle and in the 17th and 18th centuries there are reports of other members of the family doing business in St. Malo, Bordeaux, and Nantes. They may well have developed their Nantes connection out of a base in the West Indies. The Brownes' rise to considerable prominence in the colonial trade was enhanced by their business links with the Kirwans, another of the 14 Tribes of Galway. Advantages were also secured by their continual marriages down the generations to daughters of other families of the Tribes. There still stands in Eyre Square today an isolated cut-stone doorway and oriel window of the Brownes that would have graced the entrance to their ancient fortified town house in what is now Lower Abbeygate Street. Geoffrey Browne was a lawyer and was the first member of his family to live permanently at their house in the country, Castle McGarrett, where he planted vast numbers of trees in 1694. A considerable part of this estate had been lost in Cromwellian times but the Brownes were given grants of over 8,000 acres in the Acts of Settlement. The legal skills of Geoffrey Browne was an undoubted factor in their success. These skills were also employed in helping to secure the 10,000 acres belonging to Sir Francis Gore. 'Browne hath been careful of our business,' Gore wrote to a friend, 'I shall be as careful in seeing him well rewarded'.

Galway families held onto their land throughout the 17th century and, by accommodating themselves to the times, were able to retain a higher proportion of their properties than the old landed families of any other county. There was a remarkable continuity between the 17th and 18th centuries, to a degree unknown in the rest of Ireland, and land and trade remained dominated by the same families. Galway provided more avenues for its sons than any other Irish region because the clan network all over Europe and the West Indies was so diffuse. With a certain degree of organisation younger siblings could be easily placed in comfortable business positions in England, France, Spain, or various islands in the Caribbean.

The son of the Geoffrey Browne of Castle McGarrett was Colonel Dominick Browne. He married his second wife Henrietta daughter of Sir Henry Lynch, Baronet, of Castle Carra in 1754. Henrietta must have died soon after the birth of their son, Dominick Geoffrey, in 1755. In an obituary written on his father's death, also in 1755, the Colonel was described as being 'of Ashford'. He must have lived there for some time and would have been a neighbour of his father-in-law Sir Henry Lynch. Like his own father earlier at Castle McGarrett, Colonel Dominick planted hardwoods in great shelter belts all over his

Evenings on the Corrib

Ashford estate forming the basis for what was to become the most famous driven woodcock shoot in Europe. There is a stone doorway in the garden at Ashford today inscribed with Colonel Dominick's initials and the date 1738, which may have formed the front door of an earlier house. It has always been thought that Colonel Dominick built the French chateau on his father's death in 1755. It is interesting to think that maybe the original of that 'chateau' was a perfectly plain 1738 Irish Georgian box with a high hipped roof that would have been typical of the date, and similar to the other smaller Browne houses on their vast estates. The famous traveller and cartographer Daniel Augustus Beaufort wrote in his *Itinerary* for 1 October 1787:

'… we rode and walked about 2 miles to Ashford, through the deer park which is very pretty and well wooded … Mr. Browne's house is small and too much contracted behind walls and hedges, in the old style, but beautifully situated with its rear to Lough Corrib, and in front a delightful small lawn, bounded on the left by the woods of the park, and on the right by the great river that flows into Lough Corrib and divides Mayo from Galway.'

The son and heir to this branch of the Browne family, Dominick Geoffrey, was brought up by his father, the Colonel, at Ashford, and was sent on the Grand Tour. In 1775, when he was in his late teens he arrived in Paris for the coronation of King Louis XVI. His descendant, the present and 4th Lord Oranmore and Browne, has a portrait of him at that time showing a foppish, powdered

The 1st Lord Oranmore and Browne, by Sir George Hayter (1787–1860)

and bewigged young man wearing a red frock coat. Dominick's father died two years after his return in 1777. It is fascinating to think that Dominick Geoffrey might have changed the profile of the simple house at Ashford by adding a glamorous new roof such as he had admired in France. Instead of the plain Irish box, a small French chateau was then to be seen overlooking Lough Corrib.

Dominick Geoffrey became a governor of Mayo and married Margaret, the daughter and heiress of the Hon. George Browne, the 4th son of the 1st Earl of Altamont of Westport House in County Sligo. Their eldest son, also named Dominick (1787–1860) was a Member of Parliament at Westminster for 16 years being raised to the Peerage of Ireland as the 1st Baron Oranmore and Browne in 1836. He represented the County Mayo in seven parliaments at Westminster between 1814 and 1836 and each one of the elections had to be contested, proving an expensive drain on his fortune. One election cost no less than £40,000, of which £600 was spent on oranges alone for the punch served to the thirsty voters! The present Lord Oranmore and Browne, aged 98, kindly allowed us to photograph his convivial ancestor in a portrait by George Hayter (1787-1860) showing him in his ermine robes. His smiling face beams out of the picture and he is described by his descendant thus: 'he spent a lot of money and was very fond of the girls and had a very enjoyable life—until he went bust'. A piece of paper that goes with the portrait records his weight at two different periods of his life and illustrates the point—Dominick was recorded as weighing 16 stone, 7lbs at an establishment in St. James' Street in London called Berry's on 28 April 1826, aged 29. At the same establishment on 17 October 1837, aged 50, he weighed 18 stone, 5lbs! His extravagant and hospitable lifestyle at all his properties including Castle Mc Garrett in County Galway, Ashford House (as it was called then) on Lough Corrib, and in London, undoubtedly contributed to both his weight gain and his financial collapse. The failure of the potato crop in Ireland followed by the famine and the consequent lack of rents from his tenants completed his ruin, as it did for many other landlords at the time. In 1854/55 most of his Galway property which had been in the family for 600 years had to be sold in the Encumbered Estates Court. When part of his enormous estate at Ballinasloe had to be given up, the property was cattily described by Sidney Godolphin Osborne in 1850 as being 'a beautiful specimen of the effect of negligence and extravagance'.

It was only after a hard struggle that he was able to buy back a portion of his County Mayo lands and Castle Mc Garrett, the family seat. But his little gem of a shooting lodge on the shores of the Corrib and the vast acres that went with it were lost to him for ever.

At Ashford Castle today, a comfortable seat for tea overlooks the gardens

A Devastated Land

T he stone walls enclosing the small irregular fields follow every curve of the landscape and make one catch one's breath at their beauty. Round lichen-covered stones were painstakingly placed one upon another by human hands of long ago. They are balanced so that light shows between each stone and they seem almost like bands of lace.

For the visitor today these walls are the first sign on the road from Shannon airport to Ashford Castle that you are in the West of Ireland. Yet they remain as silent witnesses to a scene so terrible and so devastating that it remained seared into the memories of all who visited Counties Galway and Mayo during the years of the Great Famine, 1845–1851. During that period it is estimated that the population of Ireland was reduced by over two million people. One million died of starvation and famine-related diseases, and it is thought that more than one million emigrated. The population of Ireland was 8 million in 1845, more than double what it is today at 3.6 million. Counties Galway and Mayo were two of the worst affected regions in the country. I am indebted to the historian Kathleen Villiers-Tuthill whose book *Patient Endurance: The Great Famine in Connemara* I have plundered for many of the facts, figures, and quotations in this chapter.

The potato was so cheap and easy to grow that the poor needed little more than a plot of land in order to be self-sufficient. A man in Connemara observed to a visitor in 1844: '365 days a year we have the potato. The blackguard of a Raleigh who brought 'em here entailed a curse upon the labourer that has broke his heart. Because the landholder sees we can live and work hard on 'em, he grinds us down in our wages, and then despises us because

we are ignorant and ragged'. The majority of the peasantry lived in little one- or two-roomed cabins with thatched roofs—everything else that could be produced on the hills, the bogs, the lakes, and the shore was sold to pay the rent to the landlord. There were also middle-men or strong farmers in two-storey stone houses who had often profited from the famine. The diet of the poor consisted of potatoes and milk, varied for the better off with a little fish or bacon, oatmeal, and eggs from time to time. Their almost total dependency on the potato made their situation very vulnerable and they lived literally from one harvest to the next. There had been a steady rise in the population and, as the demand for land increased the tenants began sub-dividing their holdings. 'If a man's daughter marries they go and subdivide again. They are so fond of subdividing that their holdings will not support the number of people that creep in upon them,' reported a visitor. It was this attempt by so many near-starving people to eke out a living that explains the tracery of walls, spreading their web around ever-smaller fields, that are left behind in the Irish countryside today.

A young Scottish land agent named Thomas Colville Scott wrote in his diary: 'Every spot of soil however limited in extent, barren in productive powers, or inaccessible in

Below, A Victorian photograph showing a windswept view of the Corrib
Right, Coffee and brandy by the Inglenook fireplace at Ashford Castle today

situation, is turned up, and in many cases, beautifully tilled … no English labourer would undertake a tithe of the toil for the whole reward'. They had no money and nothing in reserve and the impact of the potato blight was immediate. Before the harvest in 1845 there were less than 1,000 paupers in all the workhouses in the whole of County Galway and the county was not considered particularly poor. In 1847 when soup kitchens had finally been set up by the government, 56,003 human beings in the same county were receiving soup.

The Rev. Duncan of Kylemore wrote to the Chief Secretary: 'Our fellow creatures are in the state of actual starvation. My residence is daily surrounded by persons entreating me with many tears to save them from dying from hunger'. In Clifden a party visiting the hotel was told by the waiter 'they are dying like dogs. One woman who had crawled the previous night into the outhouse had been found the next morning partly eaten by dogs. Another corpse had been carried up the street in a wheelbarrow, and had it not been that a gentleman accidentally passing by had given money for a coffin, it would have been thrown into the ground, merely covered with a sheet.' In Cleggan the same person declared: 'The distress was appalling far beyond my powers of description.

Left, The gardens at Ashford Castle today
Above, The Connemara landscape by Lady Ardilaun

I was quickly surrounded by a mob of men and women, more like famished dogs than fellow creatures, whose figures, looks and cries all showed that they were suffering the ravening agony of hunger.' In one cabin they found 'two emaciated men, lying at full length on the damp floor in their ragged clothes, too weak to move, actually worn down to skin and bone. In another a young man was dying of dysentery; his mother had pawned everything even his shoes, to keep him alive; and I never shall forget the resigned, uncomplaining tone with which he told me that all the medicine he wanted was food.'

Refusing to give any more gratuitous relief, as had been done in 1845, the Government decided that relief was only to be provided in return for work. In County Galway, the average number of people employed each day on Public Works (stone breaking) between 1846/1847 was 33,325. This was in stark contrast to other parts of the country —the daily average in County Donegal was 335 and in County Antrim 270. Fever broke out throughout the

county and because of all the work done on the Public Works the previous year only a tiny proportion of land was cultivated. In December 1847, eleven boatloads of paupers arrived at the Galway workhouse from Connemara where they had been evicted from one estate. The policy of eviction was widespread, particularly in the western part of the county and the local poor law inspector accused the landlords and their agents of great cruelty in destroying the houses of the poor after evicting them.

The veil of romance associated with the west of Ireland was torn away by the Great Famine, revealing a death's head landscape. Reports from Connemara were as terrible as those from anywhere in the country.

Around the world up to the present day, the bitter memories of this ecological disaster have been imprinted onto the folk memory of generations of Ireland's diaspora. Dr. R. F. Foster in his essay *Ireland After The Famine* sums up the situation: 'The general reaction was the passive one: emigration or death. The result was selective depopulation,

*The 'true rust' of the Barons' Wars—battlements on
Lough Corrib*

and the export of a race memory of horror'. By 1847 a
quarter of a million people were emigrating annually.

The Oranmore and Brownes, bankrupted by high
living and the general collapse of agricultural profits that
followed the end of the Napoleonic Wars, could only do
too little too late. The people were starving and from the
landlord's point of view these tenants were primarily a
potato-fed, rent-producing stock, which if proving non-
profitable, were to be removed post haste. Such harsh
pragmatism in the face of so much human suffering seems
unimaginable. But landlords whether good or bad, were
already bankrupt themselves, and helpless in the face of
such overwhelming tragedy.

The historian J. A. Froude noted in his essay *On the Uses
of a Landed Gentry*:

'I was staying the year before the Irish famine at a
large house in Connaught. We had a great gathering there
of the gentlemen of the county; more than a hundred of
us sat down to luncheon on the lawn. My neighbour at the
table was a Scotchman … "There," he said to me, "you see
the landed gentry of this county. In all the number there
may be one at most two, who believe that the Almighty put
them into this world for any purpose but to shoot grouse,
race, gamble, drink, or break their necks in the hunting-
field. They are not here at all for such purposes, and one
day they will find it so."' He was right, because the potato
failed the next year.

'The day of reckoning,' Froude commented dryly, 'was
nearer than he thought' and he finishes 'the whole set of
them (the county gentlemen) were swept clean away'.

George Moore explained the situation in *Parnell and His
Island*: 'For in Ireland there is nothing but land; with the
exception of a few distillers and brewers in Dublin, who
live upon the drunkenness of the people, there is no way
in Ireland of getting money, except through the peasant.
In Ireland, the passage, direct and brutal, from the horny
hands of the peasant, to the delicate hands of the
proprietor, is terribly suggestive of serfdom. In England the
landlord lays out the farm and builds the farm buildings; in
Ireland he does absolutely nothing. He gives the bare land
to the peasant and sends his agent in to collect the half-
yearly rent; in a word, he allows the peasant to keep him in
ease and luxury. In Ireland every chicken eaten, every glass
of champagne drunk, every silk dress trailed in the street,
every rose worn at a ball, comes out of a peasant's cabin.'

Father Lavelle in *The Irish Landlord Since the Revolution*
was to firmly lay the blame for the pathetic state of the
country, even before the Great Famine, firmly on the
shoulders of the big absentee landlords. These landlords
did not live on or even visit their estates, did not spend
a penny on their upkeep, and left them to be managed
unsupervised by middlemen, or agents with no supervision,
while they lived abroad off the rents from their tenants.
He records that The Marquis of Sligo, the Earl of Lucan,

The original doorway of the old Browne house at Ashford

Lord Kilmaine, Lord Arran, and Sir Roger Palmer who were all big landlords in Counties Galway and Mayo were all permanent absentees. They were paid over £100,000 annually from their rents without bothering to visit or invest in their estates in any way. Recording the state of the counties Father Lavelle notes of specific regions during the famine:

'Co. Mayo: There are 15 absentee landlords; their agents do not live in the parish and seldom come near it; no non-resident landlord has sent any subscription. The resident landlords, in some cases, are giving assistance to those around them, but no general subscription has been entered into. I, as vicar of the parish, called a meeting, but no one attended, as they said there was no one to represent the principal landlord who is an absentee. Extent 14 miles by 12. Population about 16,000.'

The effects of the famine were still being felt in Galway and Mayo well into the 1850s. The Encumbered Estates Court was a court that had been especially set up in order to be able to legally free the titles of the landed estates so that they could be sold. Most estates were burdened by the encumbrances of various family debts and hung around with responsibilities for widow's pensions, daughters' dowries, as well as the owners' own extensive overdraft. The Encumbered Estates Court freed the estates from all their legal entanglements so that their landlords could immediately put them on the market. Attempting to drum up business W. B. Webster wrote in 1853 in *Ireland Considered as a Field for Investment or Residence*:

'Assuming, as we naturally may, that the lover of a country life and the pursuit of agriculture is something of a sportsman as well, in no country, perhaps, could he meet with all the sports of the field in such perfection … Grouse abounds on nearly all mountain ranges … As a fishing country, Ireland has been justly renowned … For hounds, horses and hunting Ireland is, if possible, more famous.'

He goes on to expiate on the good land and cheap labour available:

'Labourers, 8d. to 15d. per day
Masons, 1s. to 2s. per day
Carpenters, 1/6d to 2s per day
Women, 4d.to 6d. per day!'

In industrialised Britain these words fell on the eager ears of business men as well as carpet baggers all wanting to establish themselves as country gentlemen. As soon as the old landlords withdrew from the map, estates were bought all over the West with the Berridges snapping up most of Connemara, and the Pollocks setting up an 'ideal farm'. Marrying their daughters to penurious peers the rich moved into the landed gentry in a single generation. To the devastated villagers and the countryside around Cong the unheralded arrival in their midst of Benjamin Lee Guinness was to come, in the words of Peter Campbell, 'as manna to the people'.

Chandeliers alight in the hotel's Connaught Room

Chapter 5

Stout
Salvation

*I*n 1855 'dapper, pious, spruce, and genial'
Benjamin Lee was the managing director of the
Guinness Brewery in St. James' Gate in Dublin,
the grandson of Arthur Guinness, the founder of
the Guinness dynasty and Ireland's first millionaire.

He was described in retrospect by *The Court Journal*
of 28 January 1905 as having:

'a genial refined face, like an ivory miniature, which
was so familiar to the poor of Dublin who looked
forward to seeing him as he drove daily in his quiet little
dark green brougham through the old part of the City
to his offices in Thomas Street.'

Born in 1798 his father (the second Arthur Guinness)
had taken him into the Brewery as an apprentice aged 16,
by 24 he was a partner, and by 40 the undisputed head.
Brought up under the influence of the great revivalist
preacher John Wesley who had so impressed his father,
Benjamin Lee was an intensely religious man and
considered the steadily increasing prosperity of Guinness
to be first and foremost a proof of Divine mercy. He had
grown up and into middle age under his father's stern
evangelical eye.

However, as soon as his father died, the cautious policy
of steady growth in the business was suddenly upgraded
into determined export and expansion. In a few years this
would make Benjamin Lee the richest man in the land.
The year after his father's death he bought No 80
St. Stephen's Green in Dublin, then 81, and combined the
two to create a house with 30 bedrooms, accommodation
for 20 servants, and expansive gardens. This was later
to become Iveagh House, now headquarters to the
Department of Foreign Affairs. Benjamin Lee began to

entertain on a lavish scale and the legendary Guinness hospitality was born.

The family fortune was increasing at a considerable rate and he thought of investing 'a small sum of say £20,000 to £30,000' in the purchase of land.

He had already restored St. Patrick's Cathedral in Dublin for £150,000 and was prominent in public life and in philanthropy. The Lord Lieutenant of Ireland, Lord Wodehouse congratulated him on the restoration:

'which had been too great for the Knights of St. Patrick, or for the Ecclesiastical Commissioners, or the Bench of Bishops, which the Irish Parliament had refused to undertake and which the British parliament never entertained the thought of executing, has been accomplished within four years by a single merchant.'

The Dean of St. Patrick's eulogised him thus:

'With the eye of an architect, the resources of a Prince, the public spirit of a true citizen and patriot, and above all, as an earnest practical Christian man, he has reared a temple on whose every stone and cornice, on whose every embellishment, his name might be inscribed.' It is said that one particular Cathedral window, inscribed with the text 'I was thirsty and ye gave me drink' gave successive generations of visitors great amusement. Perhaps this was an even more fitting tribute than the handsome statue that stands in the shadow of the cathedral today.

His inauguration as Lord Mayor of Dublin in 1851 was a magnificent occasion and the sumptuous civic

Left, Contrasting exotics flourish along the Terrace Walk,
giving a flavour of a once-splendid Victorian garden
Right, Maples in the garden

Sir Benjamin Lee Guinness, from an 1865 medal commemorating his restoration of St. Patrick's Cathedral

banquet attended by the Lord Lieutenant and every important dignitary in the city 20 days later reminded people of the one given 30 years earlier in honour of King George IV himself.

Not only was Mr Guinness established as Dublin's leading citizen, he was also head of its most flourishing commercial concern. Benjamin Lee Guinness had certainly departed from the simple life led by his father and grandfather. His grandfather, the first Arthur Guinness, had started his career by working for the old Archbishop of Cashel in Celbridge. His father Richard Guinness had been the 'agent and receiver' and, it is said, invented the delicious black brew that had made the old ecclesiastic a favourite with the local gentry. The Archbishop in his will left Richard and his son Arthur £100 each—the father, Richard, started a famous coaching inn at Leixlip, and the son started his first Brewery at the age of 21. All that was needed to seal the 110-year metamorphosis from Protestant trades people to the landed gentry was a country estate and a title.

Benjamin Lee married his first cousin, the deeply religious and low church Elizabeth Guinness in 1837. They enjoyed an exceptionally happy marriage and had four children—Anne, who married Lord Plunket Archbishop of Dublin; Arthur Edward (later Lord Ardilaun); Benjamin Lee; and Edward Cecil (later the 1st Earl of Iveagh). Their youngest son, Edward Cecil, would become the next head of the Brewery and the greatest philanthropist of his age in either Ireland or England. Benjamin Lee's wife, Elizabeth, known as Bessie, had never been taken in by the flashy and fashionable society in which they were now the established leaders, but she was never sure of her husband and lived in daily fear for his eternal soul.

Bessie worried desperately about what would happen to him if she was to die and wrote to her young son Arthur Edward advising him how to act if she was no longer there:

'Do, my darling, avoid bad company, I mean worldlings, for there will be plenty anxious to come here, and do guard darling papa from designing worldly women, for he will be much set on and might easily be taken in. I do not mean that he should not marry, but that he will get one who will help him on to that future world and not lead him to think of or live for the present.'

Her fears, however, proved groundless because when she died her husband did not marry again but took to political life instead.

Work, discipline, and duty were what mattered, and a concerted effort to get Ireland back on her feet after the Famine by providing ample employment with fair remuneration. Christian duty implied responsibility to the workforce. Like the Quakers, Benjamin Lee was a benevolent employer, providing job security, pensions, decent housing and amenities. Wages were higher than in any other company and a job at the Guinness brewery was gold indeed.

Chapter 5

Bessie divided her time between their town house on St. Stephen's Green, and country house at St. Annes, Clontarf. We do not know what she thought of her husband's purchase in 1852 of Ashford House and its acres on the edge of Lough Corrib.

Her husband had first come to Cong as an amateur archaeologist fascinated by the Abbey and its antiquities. As soon as he realised Ashford was for sale and saw the beautiful view and all the possibilities for improvement offered by the islands, the shooting, the fishing, and the land, he bought the entire estate as soon as he could.

The effects of the Famine were still being felt in the locality and there was desolation all around. A massive tree planting scheme was undertaken around the estate. Benjamin Lee pulled down, with the owners' consent, many of the rotting cottages and rebuilt, on better ground, sound, well-roofed houses for his tenants. Roads were built, land drained, farming begun, trees planted, and upwards of 300 people were employed on his improvement schemes, including the restoration of the Royal Abbey of Cong, and the rescuing of some of the scattered antiquities of the area.

Below, The coat of arms of Lord Ardilaun, eldest son of Sir Benjamin Lee Guinness
Opposite, The medieval cloisters at Cong Abbey that so fascinated Sir Benjamin Lee Guinness when he first came to Cong in the early 1850s

Chapter 5

The curved beak and sharp talons of eagle and falcon on a gloved fist

What was to become the world-famous woodcock shoot was re-activated and Benjamin Lee took a keen and constant interest in the running of every part of his new estate at Ashford.

Henry Coulter recorded his opinion of Benjamin Lee Guinness in his book, *The West of Ireland* (1862):

'… the position he occupies here is so important, and the good he is doing so great, both in extent and character, as to justify more than a mere passing notice. Mr. Guinness is the largest landed proprietor in the district, the several estates he has acquired within the last 12 years comprising about 9,000 Irish acres.

'He first became the purchaser of the Ashford estate, immediately adjoining the village from Lord Oranmore, and subsequently bought the Doonas estate from Sir Richard O'Donnell, and Cong estate from Mr. Alexander Lambert, and lastly he purchased the Ross-hill estate, the joint property of the Earls of Charlemont and Leitrim. He has thus become owner of a large tract of land extending from the shores of Lough Corrib to those of Lough Mask, besides having property beyond Maam and in other places. Mr. Guinness has displayed as a landed proprietor the same energy, enterprise, judgment, and liberality, that characterise the management of the gigantic commercial establishment over which he presides.

'He found the Ashford estate in a most neglected condition, with an impoverished tenantry, living in those miserable and filthy hovels that are so great an eyesore and disgrace to the country. The land adjoining the house had also been much neglected …'

Coulter goes on to explain how it has been cleared of stones, drained and cultivated and converted into good meadow land:

'Mr. Guinness took a large number of the tenants' holdings into his demesne, which he has enclosed by a well-built stone wall; but the tenants thus dispossessed have been compensated by obtaining equally large, and in some

Fishing on the Corrib

cases larger, holdings of better land on another part of the estate, so that they will benefit by the change. Mr. Guinness is trying the experiment of improving the taste and habits of his tenantry by erecting good substantial dwelling houses for them … The new houses are two stories high, slated, very neat in appearance. They are also let at a very low rent which the writer considers could be greatly increased if the benevolent landlord was to ask the equivalent rent that was generally being asked for the same land in other parts of the county.'

He continues:

'It would be difficult for me to enumerate all the improvements which Mr. Guinness has effected and all the good he has done since he became the owner of these estates. He has made roads, built largely, reclaimed much land, planted extensively; and the amount of employment which he has thus afforded to his tenants and the labouring population generally, has been very considerable. He has thus been the means of relieving much destitution in the country.'

The author is in no doubt that if his example were followed by other large employers 'no cry of distress would emanate from Cong and its vicinity … He also allows his tenants to collect brushwood for fuel from his woods at Ballykine, and has charted a large boat to bring coal down the Corrib for anyone who needs it.'

Like all proprietors of Ashford Benjamin Lee could not resist improving the building itself. The untiringly observant Coulter reports:

'He allowed a portion of the old house to remain, and built extensive additions to it, so as to form a spacious and comfortable edifice.'

In a drawing in Coulter's book we can see the original house with its high roof and two enormous chimneys and what appears to be a secondary long-gabled wing joining it to the original tower.

Perhaps because he had so much to do and because Bessie did not visit very often we do not hear reports of the lavish entertaining enjoyed in town. So began a new era at Ashford House as Benjamin Lee Guinness applied the same principles of energetic care, attention to detail, and astute judgement to the running of his estate as he did to the running of his business. As a result, the countryside around Cong flourished.

In 1865 Benjamin Lee was elected MP to represent the City of Dublin in the House of Commons at Westminster in 1865 and created a Baronet in 1867. His wife's fears were never realised. After her death, he did not take up with fast and worldly women but caught a chill after a late sitting at the House. He died peacefully in 1867, his goals in life achieved and safe in the knowledge that the future of his eternal soul was probably secure.

A lakeside view with the old Browne house on the extreme right

Chapter 6

Establishing an Estate

*A*rthur Edward Guinness, the eldest son of such
a worthy sire was born in 1840 and had been
visiting Ashford and staying there during the
summer holidays ever since his father
purchased it for him in 1852. Sir Benjamin Lee first
bought the 1,179 acres known as the Ashford Estate in the
Parish of Ross through the Encumbered Estates Court.
Sold as Lots 22 and 23 of the Oranmore Estate, Ashford
comprised eleven town lands at a cost of £11,005 and
was bought in Trust by his agent William Burke for
Arthur Guinness.

Arthur enthusiastically encouraged his father's interest
in the buying of the Ross Hill estate in Joyce's Country
in north-west Galway (so-called because a race of Welsh
giants called Joyce settled there in the 14th century).
A total of 13,595 Irish acres were put up for sale jointly by
the 3rd Earl of Leitrim and the 3rd Earl of Charlemont
and were acquired by the Guinnesses out of a total estate
of 22,550 acres.

Early in 1800, the 2nd Earl of Leitrim who 'was a man
of cultured mind and literary tastes and formed a valuable
library chiefly connected with the history and antiquities
of Ireland' had married Mary Bermingham. She was elder
daughter and co-heiress of William Bermingham (d.1798)
of Ross Hill on Lough Mask, County Mayo and in 1802
her sister Anne married the 2nd Earl of Charlemont. The
children of the sisters therefore found the Landed Estates
Court sale a cheap and convenient means of dividing their
mother's Bermingham inheritance. Lord Charlemont took
his half in cash and Lord Leitrim retained his half of the
land and bought up most of Lord Charlemont's as well.
Lord Leitrim records on 15 August 1860 'An interview

with Mr. Guinness that was unsatisfactory,' but on 17 February 1861 he crows 'Got my money for The Ross Hill estate'. This suggests that Mr. Guinness changed his mind and privately bought some additional land.

In speaking about the sisters who were the mothers of the two young Earls, the authoress Lady Morgan said that she had never seen 'two such beautiful creatures as the Berminghams, the youngest the loveliest of the two.'

Lady Russell recorded in her book *Mano's Memories and Memoranda* that Thomas Moore the poet wrote from Milan in 1819 about Anne Bermingham, the future Lady Charlemont: 'the effect she produces here with her beauty is wonderful. Last night at the Countess of Albany's the Italians were ready to fall down and worship her.'

Lord Byron said of her: 'Oh! that face! to be beloved by that woman I would build and burn another Troy.'

In 1803/4 Lady Leitrim was described as having 'a very animated affection' for the house at Ross Hill and the decision was taken not to let it, because the estate would benefit from the at least occasional residence of the family. The co-heiresses' mother Mrs. Bermingham, expressed a wish in 1825 that her daughters would continue to use the house after her death. However, after she died in 1826 and later after Lady Leitrim's death in 1840 it was probably let

or abandoned. By 1865 only one wing of the Bermingham house was still standing and the 3rd Earl built himself a cottage at Derry Park, a detached portion of the estate. He nevertheless relied on the hotel at Maam Bridge for accommodation when he visited his property.

At the end of September 1865, the 3rd Earl's brother-in-law Ynyr Burges and his daughter Alice visited Ross Hill, as recorded in Burges' diary:

'28 September. Started from Clifden for Maam. The drive through the mountains was perfect Connemara scenery, the Twelve Pins before us. The rocky precipices looked as if they would close over us every moment, and the masses of rocks, indistinctly seen appeared like bandittis standing close to us. On we went through this romantic pass. At last, one solitary light cheered us at a distance. By degrees we neared it, which proved to be the small hotel at Maam. I shall never forget my feelings of doubt whether we would find a night's lodging here or not. The fates decided that all was in our favour. Two maids received us at the door and conducted us to a comfortable room. There we supped and reposed in the most welcome apartments, after a very severe day and night's travelling.'

The Maam hotel is now called Keane's pub, and was originally built by Alexander Nimmo, the great engineer

THE BALL-ROOM IS READY IN TIME,

THE GUESTS COME AT HALF-PAST NINE.

GRAND SUPPER AT ONE.

WE DANCED TILL THE SUN

DID NOT, THOUGH IT OUGHT TO DID, SHINE.

WE HAD FIREWORKS, TOO, IN THE PARK,

THE NIGHT WAS UNCOMMONLY DARK,

THE PERFORMER WAS SKILLED,

SO NO ONE WAS KILLED.

THE NEIGHBOURS ENJOYED MUCH THE LARK.

Above, below and overleaf,
Scenes from a A Lay
of Ashford, *by Colonel*
James O'Hara

THE STEAMER TO GALWAY HE SENDS,
TO BRING UP HIS NUMEROUS FRIENDS,
MY LORD, AND MY LADY,
B. O'H., AND HER BABY,
AND "PATTI" HER SERVICES LENDS.

The wedding of Lord and Lady Ardilaun at Bantry House

who built many of the roads in this part of the country and all over Ireland. Ynyr Burges did not mention the most notorious controversy surrounding this hotel, a controversy with which his own brother-in-law, the 3rd Earl of Leitrim (later murdered because of his brutality to his tenants on his Donegal estates) was involved. The Earl refused to allow his enemy the 7th Earl of Carlisle and Lord Lieutenant of Ireland to enter the hotel in 1863 when he was on a tour of the West of Ireland. The Viceregal party had to press on to Cong, where the hostelry that received them bears to this day the name The Carlisle Arms.

Ynyr Burges' diary continues:

'29 September. Went on to Cong. A great mountain drive, which ended in the softer scenery of Lough Corrib. Arrived at The Carlisle Arms, and walked about Mr. Guinness' grounds and all through the old abbey. In an angle we were shown the tomb of Thomas Bermingham, son of John Bermingham of Lough Mask, the great grandfather of my wife …'

They visited the old Ross Hill house:

'It was here Lady Leitrim [his mother-in-law] and Lady Charlemont, the beauties of their day, passed their childhood. Alas! all empty now. No inmate but an old follower of the family, who takes care of one remaining wing of the mansion, with tears in her eyes, is left to give any account of an ancient race that were most respected in times gone by.'

On his father's death in 1868 Arthur Guinness was 28 years old. He inherited the Baronetcy, the place he loved best, Ashford House, and St. Annes, the charming villa outside Dublin. He also inherited, in equal shares with his younger brother, Edward Cecil, the Guinness Brewery. Within a couple of years of his father's death, the new Sir Arthur Guinness must have held a house party at Ashford, inviting all the neighbours..We know this because, as I walked around the hotel looking for a clue to unlock the past, I came across a room hung with line drawings. These are witty caricatures accompanied by doggerel verses composed and drawn by Colonel James O'Hara of Lenaboy, County Galway.

Dedicated to 'Sir A. G.' they begin:

'A Baronet lived by a lake,
In a house he's about to forsake,
He was cheery and hearty,
So he got up a party,
The echoes of Ashford to wake.'

A caricature of a proud and dapper-looking Sir Arthur boasts a huge spruce head, whiskers, little moustache and bowler hat, arms crossed and gazing out across the lake where his steam launch *The Eglinton* is at rest, while in the background a very recognisable Ashford House with chimneys and gables is drawn.

And so we are taken through the weekend—a ballroom is being built by workmen in enormous carpenters' hats, Arthur's brother the tiny Captain Lee Guinness, is there in full guard's uniform with his very tall servant from 'the Blues'.

Lord Ardilaun

Figures dance, the steam launch goes to Galway to fetch more friends, ladies arrive and are teased:

'I seldom a compliment pay
But to Maud B. I feel that I may,
She's as "neat quite as paint",
And fair as a saint,
And wears her own hair they all say'

One of the ladies danced with the future Edward VII:

'Danced with a Prince,
Whom she hasn't seen since'!

James O'Hara's own wife and baby are also mentioned:

'B.O'H. wouldn't leave her dear Bab
With its nose so resembling its Dad
Who'd ever have thought it
She really brought it
Some said she was cool, others, mad.'

The drawings are piercingly sharp and clever — the ladies have long spiky eyelashes and neatly coiled, glossy hair and are perfectly dressed with tiny waists and tiny shoes peeping out from beneath their skirts.

The launch, smoke billowing from the funnel is loaded with huge trunks and smiling guests, with the Baronet up front in charge, as it steams down Lough Corrib. The Master of the Galway Blazers gazes at some charming foxes who sit up and beg, and at one point everyone chases 'the rhymester' who throws himself into the Lough and he then has to dry his clothes by his bedroom fire.

Guests go on a picnic, the boat goes aground, someone hides the champagne and sherry, someone else catches the train for Cork rather than Cong, a couple go for a row on the Lough in a very small boat, Lord and Lady John Manners and Henry Manners go for a moonlit walk, Algernon Persse of Roxburgh who married the Hon. Norah Gough from Lough Cutra stands proudly next to some curious-looking cattle, the ballroom is finally ready, the splendidly pompous Liddells band comes down from Dublin:

'The band came from Dublin to play
At dinner, and dancing each day,
The leader was fat
Behold how he sat,
As he strummed in his grandiose way.'

The ball takes place with a wonderful assortment of figures waltzing determinedly. The following day the weeping Baronet sees off his friends from his steps as they board the steam launch The Eglinton, equipped with enormous pocket hankies as their huge initialled trunks are heaved on board:

'Tis the last day, no wonder we moan,
The Boat waits to take us all home,
It blows a whole gale,
Our faces grow pale,
We return to our cold mutton bone.'

Somehow, I have been lent a chart to the drawings, and I know the tiny guardsman is the youngest brother, Captain Lee Guinness, and the lawyer dancing in his wig is David Plunket (later Lord Rathmore), Lord and Lady Clanmorris are there, Mr. Algernon Persse, and

Good weather brings out the sail boats on Lough Corrib

*A watercolour (c. 1860)
showing the old Oranmore
and Browne house, with
Sir Benjamin Lee Guinness'
additions on either side*

Mrs. Burton and Miss Attie Persse of Moyode, with the Hon. Maude Bingham daughter of the Clanmorrises (later Mrs. Allen Brassey), and Miss Alice Eyre of Eyrecourt (later Mrs Miller), Mr. Frank Joyce, and a Captain McAlpine of 'the Blues'.

Colonel James O'Hara of Lenaboy (1832–1902) is certainly an unsung gifted caricaturist. There are two other heavenly albums of hilariously captioned drawings by him of other cruises with friends that he took, one to Iceland in the *Mary* and one to Greece in the *Caroline*. I am most grateful to Bernard Williams for lending me the original book, *A Lay of Ashford*, which is very rare and was privately printed. On the green cover etched in gilt is a fascinating picture of Ashford House seen from the Lough as it must have appeared then. The high hipped roof has two pediments, stone urns at the four corners, and in the centre between the two little pediments, the stone eagle which was the Sligo crest. It is similar to those on the parapet of Westport House and as the mother of the Ist Lord Oranmore was a Sligo Browne this possibly explains why the eagle was there, as it still is today.

The building looks just like an early 18th century Irish house and its original stone-blocked front door on the other side certainly dates from the 1730s or 1740s and is clearly shown in Sir William Wilde's illustration in his book on Lough Corrib published in 1867 and in later 19th century photographs. Both this and view of the Lough in Wilde's book show a crenellated tower with a flag flying which is mentioned in his text as being 'recently erected'.

It is unclear how much of the original de Burgo tower was left, and one suspects perhaps comparatively little for in the Ordinance Survey Map of 1841 Ashford House is clearly shown with its long straight avenue stretching ahead from the front door of the house out into the countryside for a couple of miles in the direction of Ballinrobe.

Only very faintly depicted on the map is what looks like a square-shaped structure standing on line with the house in the gardens. This must have been the remains of the original tower which then formed the basis of Sir Benjamin Lee Guinness' romantic 'feudal' tower as we can see in Sir William Wilde's book and on the cover of *A Lay of Ashford*. This gilt picture on the cover of the book shows the house when it had been given a Victorian face-lift with plate glass windows and a gabled extension. There are lots of trees between the Lough and the house, a sundial, and an informal pond, stemming from a spring where the fountain is today.

James O'Hara, later became a Lieutenant-Colonel, in command of the 5th Brigade North Irish Division Royal Artillery former Captain 2nd Dragoon Guards. He was High Sheriff and Justice of the Peace several times for Galway, so on his Ashford visit he must have been in his thirties. The whole company at Ashford were in their twenties and thirties and it must have been an enjoyable and carefree party for old friends and neighbours. It might have been one of the last bachelor jaunts for Sir Arthur Guinness before matrimony beckoned in 1871. In a way this was the group of close friends and relations that he

would keep throughout his life in Galway and they keep appearing through the story. Educated at Eton and at Trinity College, Dublin, Sir Arthur Guinness was now jointly responsible with his brother for the entire running of the Brewery. The Guinnesses were a devoted and close family, but nevertheless it had been Edward Cecil who was educated at home and who had been working in the Brewery with his father since he was 16, while Arthur had been at school and then at Trinity.

It may have been that the younger son was the father's favourite, but the business was left equally between the older and younger son. Lee, the middle soldier brother, who had already run up debts, was not included in the business. The Will had been clearly designed to ensure that the least harm should be done to the business should the partnership come to an end and the remaining partner given every chance of carrying it on.

Although an accountable 28-year-old, there is nothing to show that Arthur was interested in brewing and he was already immersed in politics, while Edward had been his father's secretary for many years. Intelligent, hard-working and ambitious, Edward Cecil had gathered a fair knowledge of how the business worked.

Arthur seems to have regarded Guinness primarily as a source of income, while his younger brother's attitude was more responsibly business-like. Edward was an excitable young man, brilliant and gay with an intense vitality, and he found collaboration with his brother extremely difficult, his own sure touch and quick decision-making often causing difficulties.

As time went on his attitude to the direction of the business became more determined and possessive. However, it was not until eight years after their father's death that Arthur finally decided to withdraw from the partnership on the very generous terms suggested by his brother. Edward Cecil became the sole proprietor. The sum of £680,000 including his half share of the year's profits was to be paid to the eldest brother over a period of four years in six instalments between 1 January 1877 and 1 August 1880. This sum together with his investments and the private fortune left him by his father made Sir Arthur Guinness a millionaire.

Meanwhile, politics had become a major interest. He was returned for his father's seat at a by-election on his death and represented the City of Dublin at Westminster. He was returned again in the General Election of 1868. Unfortunately, it was discovered that his agent had bribed an elector without his knowledge and he was unseated on a petition the following year, but then re-elected in 1874 holding the seat until April 1880 when he was raised to the Peerage as Baron Ardilaun of Ashford, his title taken from an island on the Corrib. During a turbulent era Arthur held very strong political views in favour of retaining the Union with Great Britain and against Home Rule and Repeal of the Union.

'No-one,' his brother wrote on his behalf to Isaac Butt, 'can feel more strongly a truly National desire for the advancement of Ireland materially and intellectually, we

Chapter 6

do not and cannot think this is to be achieved by Repeal ... but by the determination of the Irish nation to oblige their representatives to enforce, irrespective of party, the rights of those they represent, which they now almost entirely neglect.'

Although committed Unionists who desired as firmly as any Nationalist the betterment of Ireland, the Guinness brothers believed this could be achieved only by the conciliation of different parties and creeds and by practical measures for economic development. They did not want constitutional change or political agitation and the failure of both Ireland and Great Britain to achieve this was probably the greatest disappointment of both their lives. Arthur was an uncompromising and courageous Unionist and Conservative all his life and while he was young played an active part in political affairs. His views may have been extreme, but he worked behind the scenes while leaving little personal mark on the political spectrum.

'His speeches did not make much impression from the point of view of eloquence but they had the clearness and conciseness characteristic of the utterances of a good

Right, Portrait of Lord Ardilaun
Far right, a marble model of the bronze statue of Lord Ardilaun in St. Stephen's Green by Thomas Farrell (c. 1892) (Muckross House Collection)

One of the plates from A Lay of Ashford, *by Col. James O'Hara*

THEY HAD COME ON A TOUR TO THE WEST,

HER LAKES, AND HER "HIGHLANDS" TO TEST,

THE BOAT WENT AGROUND,

AND SOON IT WAS FOUND,

THAT NIGHT IN THE MUD SHE WOULD REST.

business man,' summed up the *Irish Times* in his obituary. Arthur would become the proprietor of two newspapers in Dublin, the *Daily Express*, and *The Evening Mail*, both of which held firm Unionist views. 'As a philanthropist' the obituary writer continued, 'he knew no politics. If an undertaking demanded his support, it had it, whether it was for Roman Catholic or Protestant, Unionist or Nationalist, as long as the cause was good.' He may have flaunted his Unionist views but his philanthropy was carried out unobtrusively.

The comfortable creed of the wealthy classes at that time was one of laissez faire because they believed it was God's will, a philosophy that encouraged their natural inclination to accept the appalling poverty of the working classes as inevitable. Not so the Guinness brothers. Some of the worst slums in Dublin were around St. Patrick's Cathedral and Bull Alley in The Liberties. The Rev. James Whitelaw rector of St. Catherine wrote:

'I have frequently surprised from 10–16 persons of all ages and sexes in a room not 15 feet square stretched on a wad of filthy straw swarming with vermin and without any covering, save the wretched rags that constitute their wearing apparel. Under such circumstances it is not extraordinary that I should have frequently found from 30 to 40 individuals in a house…'

A visitor described the buildings as 'veritable slums and stinkpots'. Arthur cleared the slums around St. Patrick's, and his brother did much to rehabilitate The Liberties.

The welfare services at the Brewery started at least 50 years before they were adopted by industry generally. The two brothers established a free dispensary for the workers and their families and in 1870 employed a doctor who would also visit with a pharmaceutical chemist as his assistant, a lady visitor, and a midwife. In 1880 there were 19,000 attendances and over 2,000 visits to homes. The firm generously supported the hospitals and Guinness

employees became the best paid and the best cared for both medically and socially, of any workers in the entire British Empire.

Sir Arthur Guinness was a pioneer of housing reform and, after leaving the Brewery, perhaps with a sigh of relief, he was able to devote his life to his main interest— the improvement of the city of Dublin. Even during the periods when he was not in parliament he always looked on the city as if it was his constituency. Guinness went about the business of giving money away because it gave him pleasure.

Again his obituary writer was to sum him up:

'He gave money away with prudence and good sense. He gave the impression of giving away money to please himself not others and in doing so he showed imagination and an unconventional sense of discrimination.'

He completed the restoration of Marsh's Library begun by his father and entirely re-built the newer buildings of the Coombe Maternity Hospital, doubling the accommodation. He cleared the slums around the cathedral, re-built the facade of the church of St. Anne in Dawson Street, and built All Saints in Raheny where the family is buried. He bought, cleared, laid out and planted St. Stephen's Green and presented it to the city, his ambition ever since he was a little boy.

He was President of the Royal Dublin Society for 16 years and was instrumental in saving it from dissolution at one point and he worked tirelessly for the suburb of Clontarf. He was also president, though not a very active one, of the Royal Irish Horticultural Society.

'He showed,' says his obituary writer again 'an infinite capacity for taking pains, and a careful balancing of the claims of justice with prudence. He combined probity, public spirit, and humility with hard headed business acumen.'

In 1872 he and his brother completely funded the hugely successful Dublin Exhibition of Arts, Industries, and Manufactures, which attracted 420,000 visitors and gave the business life of the city a great boost. He gave lavishly to Trinity College Dublin and to the Church of Ireland.

His obituary writer noted:

'He was a practical philanthropist and not just in the convenient form of writing cheques. In the laying out of the Green or the clearing of the slums round St. Patrick's there were no details too small to escape his personal observation and direction.' He played an enthusiastic part in the public life of the city and upheld the family tradition of service. The people of Dublin held him in respect and honour—when a subscription was raised to place his statue in St. Stephens Green the suggestion came from a Nationalist and the statue was unveiled by a Nationalist Lord Mayor both of whom would have held political views diametrically opposed to his.

It is one of only a few statues of an establishment figure that still remains in St. Stephens Green after the purging of nearly all the others by bombing and removal in the 1920s.

Building a Castle

*I*n all his good works Arthur Guinness was most sympathetically supported by his beautiful wife Olive whom he married in 1871. Lady Olivia White was the third daughter of the 3rd Earl of Bantry and lived at Bantry House on Bantry Bay in County Cork, having grown up at Macroom Castle, also in County Cork.

Nigel Everett has chronicled the story of Bantry House, and the family of the proud but spendthrift Earl of Bantry, with the development of Olive's gardens in his book *An Irish Arcadia*. Her father had been plain William Hedges White known as 'Billy Hawthorn' and was a genial individual who enjoyed the typical pleasures of a Victorian country gentleman. He rode, shot, spent a great deal of time on his yacht and confined his reading to the sporting pages of the newspapers. He was married to Jane Herbert of Muckross House in Killarney, County Kerry. In 1868 he inherited the title of Earl of Bantry from his brother and moved to Bantry House, only to find that the finances of his new estate were in a perilous condition.

We do not know how Arthur and Olive met, but *The Skibbereen Eagle* waxed lyrical about their wedding:

'The meed of praise and worthiness is accorded to the Lady Olive as a rich bouquet, to shed its lustre on the pathway of her future destiny. The accession of the present noble Earl to his title and estates, and the consequent residence of the family amongst us, has been a boon of no small magnitude indeed, every day has but developed their many virtues and graces. The noble ladies have been ever engaged in acts of benevolence visiting the sick and needy and dispensing good, even at the risk to their own personal safety ... the recipients are not chosen in a sectarian spirit

Chapter 7

… the overflowing bounties of the noble family who like their great exemplar, go forth doing good.'

The 3rd Earl had been much praised in the area for his 'leniency' towards tenants and the 'moderateness' of his rents. The news report continued:

'A very artistic arcade had been formed over the entrance to the church combining wreaths of ever greens and flowers surmounted by the armorial bearings of the noble family … of Lady Olive it may be said that "Even the slight hare-bell raised its gentle head, Elastic from her airy tread".'

The Skibbereen Eagle concluded that:

'Sir Arthur's princely fortune would afford means for cultivating her inherent spirit of liberality.'

There is a photograph, taken on the steps of Bantry House around the time of their engagement that shows the Earl of Bantry holding a pruning hook and gazing defiantly into the middle distance. He sports a white woolly beard and a very smart long, dark and many-pocketed tweed jacket. His daughters, the Ladies Elizabeth, Ina, Jane, and Olive White, are all wearing what look like the most wonderfully warm, long velvet dresses with long sleeves, white collars and cuffs, tightly fitting buttoned bodices, and sweeping full skirts with minute aprons.

The proud fiancé, Sir Arthur Guinness, is dressed in a velvet smoking jacket with quilted collars and cuffs, woollen plus-fours, and thick woollen socks ending in spats and polished shoes. The charming-looking boy is Viscount Berehaven—who was to become the dissolute 4th Earl of Bantry later dying childless of syphilis—gazed at anxiously by his mother sitting on the steps. Everyone's expressions are frozen as if they are holding their breath until the camera's shutter has clicked. Lady Olive is beautiful and serene, if not even slightly smug, as she stands next to her dashing beau, while the rest of the party are giving nothing away. If only this frozen moment could pass and we could see them moving and talking again.

The Ardilauns' butler, photographed in full Masonic dress

The wedding went off splendidly. The bride and her father were met at the church by her eight bridesmaids, her sisters the Ladies Ina, Jane, and Elizabeth White, Lady Emily Bernard, Lady Emma Bernard, the Hon. Miss Freke, Miss Colthurst, and Miss Cresswell. The solemn rites were performed by the Bishop of Tuam and the Rev. Godfrey Smith, domestic chaplain to the Earl of Bantry. The bride wore white satin and Brussels lace and a tiara (worth £14,000) and diamonds presented to her by the bridegroom.

The church was packed with friends and relations and most of the local gentry of County Cork attended. After the ceremony the carriage of the happy pair was unharnessed and drawn from the church to Bantry House by the soldiers of the 22nd Regiment, now stationed at Bantry, amid the cheers and shouts of the people. The bejewelled presents are listed with the givers' names, and the first night of the honeymoon was spent at Macroom Castle *en route* to London and the Continent.

The *Ballinrobe Chronicle* was not to be outdone by *The Skibereen Eagle*, and a positively rapturous account described the festivities at Cong:

'A large bonfire was erected in front of the old Abbey, which ground it appears from an inscription on the mound had been given by Sir Arthur's father Sir Benjamin Lee Guinness Bart. MP. The town was brilliantly illuminated—every house from the Carlisle Arms Hotel which was remarkably well lighted up to the lowly dwelling of the humble labourer added their quota to the refulgence thus giving evidence of the esteem in which Sir Arthur is held in the locality as a generous employer and good landlord. Dancing was kept up to a late hour, refreshments were liberally dispersed, and oft repeated cheers were given for Sir Arthur Guinness Bart and Lady Olive Guinness.

'Ashford was also the scene of festivities, the tenantry and employees being anxious to mark their esteem for the respected proprietor. In Galway the bells of St. Nicholas rang out a joyous peal, and huge bonfires were lighted in many parts of the town. The pretty steamer *Eglinton* plying between Cong and Galway was gaily decorated with flags, and fired a salute showing general rejoicing on land and water for this happy event.'

This extremely happy, though childless, marriage was the most important influence on both of their lives. It is hard to imagine nowadays the distaste of the Victorian aristocracy for any connection with 'trade', which certainly included brewing. Lady Olive and her family must have done their utmost to encourage Sir Arthur to retire from Guinness, which would have guided his decision to accept Edward Cecil's offer to dissolve the partnership shortly after getting married. This left him free to pursue his real interests of philanthropy and public life.

There was still a particular stigma attached to the brewing trade because of the periodical attacks made upon it by the Temperance Movement. George Martelli in *Man Of His Time, A Life of the 1st Earl of Iveagh* tells us that, when the respected Sir Benjamin died, a disgruntled Temperance campaigner, J. A. Mowatt, wrote a pamphlet entitled *What it is to Die a Brewer.*

Lord Ardilaun at Ashford—
a Victorian collage showing
the Abbey in the background

An unchanged view that Lady Ardilaun loved to paint with her watercolours

'He (re)-built' St. Patrick's and gained a baronetcy by it. Prior to the restoration of St. Patrick's he was little known except through his XX labels, which are the only famous literary works he has left behind; and they are read the world over with thick tongues, bloated countenances, blood-shot eyes and staggering gait.'

This pamphlet, which is a vicious attack on the funeral oration of Dr. John Gregg, Bishop of Cork wonders how Dr. Gregg could 'bless a business like brewing or distilling'.

Mowatt continues:

'Sir B. L. Guinness promoted the Niagra of intemperance down whose rapids men have been hurled in thousands, from every land under heaven; and, during the 70 years of Sir B. L. Guinness' life the thousands of souls which his drink hurried into an awful eternity form something fearful to contemplate. What useful work did he ever promote except that of multiplying widows and orphans, and fatherless street roughs, and unfortunate drunken females—all who partook of his "spirit"?'

Peers would lecture their daughters embarking on the marriage market, 'never mind the money, don't marry a brewer'. When Edward Cecil was made the 1st Earl of Iveagh and was advancing into the House of Lords in his robes, a wit quipped, 'Here comes the Beerage'. Mocked and looked down upon by certain elements in social life, the Guinnesses were determined to scale the heights of society, even as far as the Royal Family.

But first there had to be a house of sufficient grandeur to match both the size and extent of the estate and the fortune. It had to be fit to entertain the highest in the land, and to give every impression of the family's descent from ancient knights of old. Exactly the same phenomenon was occurring in Britain when, with industrial expansion, a new breed of millionaire appeared on the scene, determined to make their mark.

Dr. J. Mordaunt Crook in his book *The Rise of the Nouveaux Riches* lists their 118 great mansions and castles in England and Scotland—in Ireland there were just three. In Britain wool brokers, chemical magnates, bankers, coal owners, brewers, ship-owners, guano millionaires, carpet kings, China traders, India merchants, copper magnates, brewers, haberdashers, even a mustard magnate all put their money into land and architecture.

Benjamin Disraeli wrote in 1845:

'In a commercial country like England, every half century develops some new vast source of public wealth, which brings into national notice a new and powerful class. A couple of centuries ago, a Turkey merchant was the great creator of wealth; the West India Planter followed him. In the middle of the last century appeared the Nabob. These characters in their zenith in turn merged into the land, and became English aristocrats. The expenditure of the revolutionary war against France produced the Loanmonger, who succeeded the Nabob; and the application of science to industry developed the Manufacturer, who in turn aspires to be "long acred", and always will, as long as we have a territorial constitution; a better security for the

The beautiful Lady Ardilaun standing between her two sisters

Edward Clifford's pre-Raphaelite portrait of Lady Ardilaun as a young woman

Lady Ardilaun photographed in her conservatory

preponderance of the landed interest than any corn-law, fixed or fluctuating.'

'By the mid Victorian period,' wrote Mordaunt Crook, 'It seemed possible to buy gentility more easily than ever before. Even so, full acceptance was slow.'

Anthony Trollope described Mr. Longestaff as a member of the old order in *The Way We Live Now*:

'He was immensely proud of his position in life, thinking himself to be immensely superior to all those who earned their bread. There were, no doubt, gentlemen of different degrees, but the English gentleman of gentlemen was he who had land, and family title deeds and an old family place, and family portraits … and family absence of any employment.'

In Ireland, a non-industrialised country, just three new millionaires appeared in the latter part of the 19th century and built the *de rigeur* cut-stone castles of Kylemore Abbey in County Galway, Ashford Castle in County Mayo, and

Glenveagh Castle in the highlands of Donegal. This was compared to dozens and dozens of similar castles in the highlands of Scotland built at the same time.

The plans at Ashford started to take shape in 1873. James Franklin Fuller was the architect, and £41,000 was spent on the building by 1875 and £1 million by 1915.

In his 1994 book, *Architecture in Ireland 1837–1921*, Jeremy Williams explains:

'Fuller had started off on excellent terms with his client, since as a genealogist he had proved that Sir Arthur was descended seven times from Alfred the Great, and as such Ashford was designed as an appropriate retreat.'

It appears, however, that the client/architect relationship deteriorated. Possibly Fuller was a little high handed and considered he knew best.

'Fuller ruefully admitted in his memoirs that he saw no reason to treat the ultra rich with awe,' says Williams. Speaking too frankly may have been his downfall, and he

Oriel turret in the garden

An early view of Ashford Castle shows the scaffolding on the 19th century building

Lady Ardilaun's sketch for a gateway to the Castle

was soon replaced by the architect George Ashlin. Ashlin had previously taken over from S. U. Roberts in the building of Kylemore Abbey in County Galway for Mitchell Henry, a textile industrialist of Irish background and based in the midlands of England.

Peter Campbell, the retired forester at Ashford Castle, today, tells us that stone masons were brought in from all the adjoining counties. In the Quantity Surveyor's accounts between 1873 and 1885 various names were associated with the work being done at Ashford.

There is the architect's firm of George Ashlin & Samuel Roberts (who had also worked at Kylemore), the surveyor was the firm of Patterson & Kempster; John Semple was the builder in 1873 with lead work supplied by Ross & Murray in 1874, plastering by James Hogan & Sons, tiling by Sibthrope & Sons, and cut-stone work by Michael O'Brien.

Forming the New Hall in the Old House is listed as being done by Henry Sharpe, builder, between 1875 and 1877. Sharpe took down the Old Billiard Room and formed the New Back Stairs. There must have been an estimate for panelling the ceilings of the New Hall, and prices for Portland Stone work in the interior of the Circular Turret. Sundry cut stone work and wood

carving are listed as being carried out by A. P. Sharp on 1 November 1877.

The limestone balustrades in the garden were executed by P. Foy, who came from a family of well-known masons in the locality. In 1884/5 the Demesne and Fence Walls along New Road were constructed by Darby Hain and Darby Murphy. The North Entrance Lodge was constructed by J. & W. Beckett.

There are surveyors' notes rejecting the North Entrance Loop and Gateway and the proposed substitute of Circular Turret for Square Tower.

Williams comments:

'Ashlin's contribution is stylistically distinguishable only by a smoother finish and sharper detailing as in the six arched battlemented bridge leading to a gatehouse dominated by a coroneted "A" commemorating Sir Arthur's elevation to the peerage as Lord Ardilaun.'

Douglas Scott Richardson in *Gothic Revival Architecture in Ireland* tells us that:

'The castle began as a block connecting an early 18th century house to the east with two closely spaced towers of an old De Burgo castle to the west … The tops of the ruined towers were rebuilt, not noticeably sympathetically, to form the north-west corner of the new castle.

Sir Arthur Guinness' yacht, The Eglinton, bedecked with flags

'The castle itself took almost nothing from the towers stylistically, not even the choice of material. On the contrary, after the new castle was built, menacing battlements were added to the old towers. There are also several stairs under long receding stone roofs, always balanced against the corbelled projection of an oriel window or some other feature.

'The detailing is Godwinian, with its many trefoiled windows, including some that are panelled blind, and even a round tower stair way. But at no time does this detailing take itself seriously as a means of defense. It contents itself with making threatening little gestures with blind loop-holes that look heavily machined and highly decorative.

'In fact, the whole castle is as obviously ornamental as those of the early 19th century, though organised visually along Mid-Victorian picturesque principles and executed with High Victorian gusto. The old house was maladroitly refaced and cleverly gutted to form an impressive group of principal rooms (the only interiors of any interest)'.

Richardson goes on to explain why the taste for Gothic Revival was beginning to change in England in the 1870s:

'By then, Gothic was "too earnest, too strong, too provincial, too gloomy, too religious." But, if anything, the

The Ardilaun coat of arms

Irish Baronial monuments which seem so grand, tough and strong by themselves, look contrived, soft and yielding next to the stumps of ancient towers, which dot the countryside'.

Of course these castles were not for defence but for decoration. They were stage sets and served a flattering purpose in linking their owner with the distant past of his family. Everyone, including the owner himself was aware that they were spectacular status statements of the day. But they are nonetheless interesting for that. For anyone wanting to see a truly prodigious ruin of the period, a visit to Dromore Castle in County Limerick built for Lord Limerick by the architect Edward William Godwin in 1866 is well worth the drive.

The building that had been known as Ashford House was now to evolve into Ashford Castle, embracing if not almost smothering the original Norman tower of the de Burgos. The massive building project continued for all of Lord Ardilaun's life. He continually thought of improvements and was extremely practical in all his ideas, even generating his own electricity from the river.

'He pressurised the water into taps, never heard of before that in the West of Ireland,' explains Peter Campbell in awe. He also showed extreme foresight in making provision for the laying of sewage pipes under the gardens and then incorporating them through the bridge, so they could be connected up without the need for any further excavation. The river is only a mile long and the temperature always low having percolated through the cavernous limestone on its way from Mask to Corrib, which is very good for fishing because low temperature water is better for fish

Below, Menus from Lady Ardilaun's dinners at Ashford Castle

When he had the bridge built he also constructed the fountain. Peter Campbell points out:

'The lights of the castle were reflected into the fountain. Fish in those days were jumping into the boats nearby.'

Peter Campbell believes that Lord Ardilaun was a very independent and private character. Of the 25 miles of roads that he built at Ashford, five were constructed in tunnels under the main roads thus masking the user from the public eye. This could also have been a safety consideration at the height of the Land War. Four of the tunnels were constructed for vehicles and one for pedestrians—again he showed foresight and built the roads wide enough to accommodate the horseless carriage that was bound to come later. Lord Oranmore and Browne's broad leaf trees on the estate were thickened out by the planting of conifers such as Monterey pines, Lawsons cyprus, Bishops pines, and Western red cedar. Laurel gave great cover for game birds and for many years the name of Cong was synonymous with the woodcock. Lord Ardilaun planted over one million trees on 3,000 acres and the planting was all finished by 1880. All the woods were planted to produce timber and the necessary shelter for game birds for his driven woodcock shoot. He built a wooden chalet with a cut-stone fireplace and thatched roof on the banks of Lough Corrib opposite the island of Ardilaun. In 1905 the Prince of Wales, soon to be King George V, was photographed with guns, loaders, and beaters spreading in a great crowd either side of him outside the chalet on one of the momentous days of his visit to shoot the woodcock. This historic occasion was to be the happy fulfilment of his host's long-cherished dream.

Ashford 1880

MENU DU 2 OCTOBRE, 1880.

POTAGES: La Paysanne au Consommé.
Crème de Riz à la Caroline.

POISSONS: Turbot Bouilli, Sauce Hollandaise.

ENTREES: Vol au Vent à la Financière.
Tournedos Piqués Sautés au Madère.
Salade de Homards en Bordure.

RELEVES: Selle de Mouton Montagnard Rotie.
Dindonneaux Farcis aux Truffes.

Punch au Vin de Bordeaux.

ROT: Cailles Bardées en Croûtes.

ENTREMETS: Baba au Rhum.
Suédoises de Pommes à la Mogador.
Sardines à la Diable.

DESSERT: Glaces Vanille et Pistaches.

MENU DU 3 OCTOBRE, 1880.

POTAGES: Le Consommé à la Pluche.
Purée de Celeris à l'Espagnole.

POISSONS: Barbue Bouillie, Sauce Crevettes.

ENTREES: Pains de Foie Gras à la Lucullus.
Cotelettes de Mouton à la Vicomtesse.
Suprêmes de Volaille à l'Ecarlate.

RELEVES: Aloyau de Bœuf Rôti à l'Anglaise.
Poulardes Braisées à la Perigueux.

Punch au Vin de Champagne.

ROT: Levreauts Rotis, Sauce Groseilles.

ENTREMETS: Pudding Diplomate au Sambayon.
Gateaux Fourrés à la Crème d'Amandes.

Pailles au Parmesan

DESSERT: Glace au Chocolat.
Glace aux Sirop de Framboises.

Chapter 8

Troubled Times

*H*owever idyllic was the Prince of Wales' visit in 1905, when Lord Ardilaun's only thoughts were for the twists and turns of his woodcock and the comfort of his royal guest, life as a landlord at Ashford was not always quite so carefree.

Michael Davitt, the inspiring founder of the Land League, was born in Mayo at the height of the famine in 1846 the son of an evicted small tenant. The historian T. W. Moody in his essay *Fenianism, Home Rule, and the Land War 1850–1891* (of which the following paragraphs are a resumé) tells his life story. The Davitt family was exiled from Mayo to Lancashire and, by the age of 9, Davitt was working 12 hours a day in a cotton mill. He lost his arm in a machine at the age of 11, which led to four years of unexpected schooling and employment with the local postmaster. In 1865 he threw himself into the Fenian movement and served seven years of a 15-year sentence in Dartmoor prison in England, before being released in December 1877 as a part of a long and persistent agitation for amnesty for Fenian prisoners by Parnell and Butt. Passionate and proud, he was also self-critical and self-disciplined. In 1878 he travelled to America where, in collaboration with John Devoy, the dominant personality among American Fenians, he formulated a new policy for the national movement—a 'new departure' that was an alliance of revolutionary and constitutional nationalists on the two great issues of self-government and land. In the winter of 1878/9 an economic crisis threatened the rural population with a disaster comparable to the Great Famine. The falling prices due to the importation of cheap American grain, crop failures, and exceptionally wet weather meant that a multitude of small farmers could not

A watercolour of a typical Galway cottage by Lady Ardilaun

pay their rents and were facing bankruptcy, starvation, and eviction.

In April 1879 Davitt joined James Daley, editor of *The Connaught Telegraph* and a number of local Fenians in organising a 'Land Meeting' at Irishtown in his native Mayo, an event that precipitated a general agitation in the West. He founded the Irish National Land League and the brilliant politician Charles Stewart Parnell became its president. The League had powerful backing from all sections of Irish nationalist opinion in America—even bishops and parish clergy were behind the League. It worked in part as a relief agency, organising the work of the voluntary relief organisations that helped to avert a second famine in the winter of 1879/80. Fair rent, fixity of tenure, and freedom for the tenant to sell his interest in his holding were the cornerstones of the crusade. The League's goal was to organise resistance to the landlords, prevent eviction and seek a reduction in rents for the ultimate purpose of transforming tenant farmers into owners of their holdings.

Moral force warfare was developed. Process serving and evictions were made the occasion of great popular demonstrations. Families evicted for non-payment of rent were sheltered and supported and an embargo was placed on evicted farms. Persons involved in prosecution because of their Land League activities were defended and families of prisoners cared for. Boycott, the terrible weapon of social ostracism (named after Captain Boycott) was perfected as the ultimate sanction of the League against all persons who violated its code.

Captain Charles Boycott, who added this new word to the English language, was a neighbour at Ashford and lived at Lough Mask House in County Mayo. He defied the Land League and as a consequence in September 1880 he and his family were reduced to a state of isolation and helplessness from which they were rescued only by a relief expedition of fifty volunteer Orange labourers from Monaghan protected by strong forces of troops. Some £350 worth of potatoes and other crops were thus harvested at a cost of over ten times their value and a humiliated Captain Boycott left the country.

For the first time, tenant farmers stood up as a class to the landlords. The passions aroused by the Land League inevitably erupted into violence and outrage, but, because the Land League was technically a lawful organisation, the government had great difficulty in coming to grips with it. The Land War of 1879–82 was the greatest mass movement of modern Ireland. As a result, The Land Act of 1881 progressively diminished the landlord's interest in the land, and dual ownership of the land paved the way for peasant proprietorship.

Gerard Moran has written an essay arguing that the activities of the minority of Irish landlords tainted all Irish landlord–tenant relations. The attempts of some landowners to improve the lives of their tenants has been generally neglected, in an attempt to classify all landlords as rack-renting, evicting murderers. It is often conveniently overlooked that the Land League leadership in Mayo in

Lady Ardilaun and a shooting party

Arriving in style at Ashford

An Irish country woman, by Lady Ardilaun

the initial stages of that agitation, urged the tenants to pay their rents to those landlords who did not extract an exorbitant rent from them and who treated them in a fair manner. It is only in recent years that historians such as W. E. Vaughan have argued that Irish landlords cannot be regarded as a homogeneous group, and the activities attributed to this class were not the standard practice of all landlords. Nevertheless, in the progress towards Irish nationhood, good and bad landlords were to become the discarded husks of a once-ruling caste.

W. E. Vaughan in *Landlords and Tenants in Ireland 1848–1904* explains that the mass demonisation of landlords that occurred after the terrible behaviour of predatory property owners such as John George Adair in Donegal, William Scully, and the 3rd Earl of Leitrim led to the generalisation that all landlords were bad. On careful scrutiny of the evidence, it has actually now become difficult for historians to find signs of them at all.

He explains:

'When systematic research began, changes in interpretation came so quickly and so effectively that it became difficult to understand how the old ideas had such power'.

Fortunately for us and our hero, Gerard Moran in his essay 'Sir Arthur Guinness and his Estate at Ashford Castle 1868–1882' in *Landlord and Tenant Relations in Ireland*, Sir Arthur Guinness and his Estate at Ashford Castle, 1868–1882 proves a case in point:

'Until recently,' he writes, 'the activities and estate management of Irish landlords has been harshly treated by most Irish historians. The excesses and mass clearance of a number of notable individuals such as the Marquis of Sligo, Lord Lucan, Sir Roger

Palmer, Lord Plunket (Lord Ardilaun's brother-in-law), and others, have tended to distort the overall picture regarding landlord–tenant relations. The activities of a number of their peers have tainted all Irish landlords'. 'The Guinness estate consisted of 25,341 acres situated in Dublin, Wicklow, Galway and Mayo. The Galway estate comprised 19,944 acres with 3,266 in Mayo, centred in the parishes of Cong and Clonbur. There were 670 tenants on the estate who paid an annual rental of £12,000. Most of the farms were between 15 and 25 acres and rents ranged from 5/- to 40/- an acre, the holdings in Galway being more expensive. Guinness was regarded by his peers and his nationalist adversaries as an improving landlord, expending large amounts of money on drainage, pier construction, cottage construction, afforestation, and other tasks, which improved the circumstances of his tenants. About 400 labourers and artisans were directly employed by him, being paid 8/- to 10/- per week. Compared with tenants and labourers in other regions of the west of Ireland, few of the tenants had to migrate annually in search of work. Many of these were employed in the extension and maintenance of Ashford House, the landlord's residence which afterwards became known as Ashford Castle. During times of major distress Guinness was renowned for his charity to his tenants, as in 1879

The schoolhouse for estate workers' children at Ashford, with the 18th century gates of the Browne house

when 3,000 pounds was provided for the purchase of meal. He prided himself on looking after his tenants and induced the poorer ones to decline aid from the relief committees. This had the effect of making his tenants more dependent on him and he was able to exercise more control over them during periods of agitation. Sir Arthur's benevolence was not confined to the Cong/Clonbur region but extended to the whole of south Mayo-north Galway region. It was his intention to open the region to tourism and with this in mind he maintained a steamer service on Lough Corrib between Cong and Galway. He was also one of the leading proponents of the plans to establish a railway line from Claremorris to Ballinrobe, investing over 10,000 pounds in the company.'

Nevertheless, opportunities were found to criticise him despite the many improvements carried out on the estate and Moran tells us:

'These [critics] became more vocal during the Land League agitation when all landlords were categorised as being bad.'

Various grumbles were raised, such as he had ended the thriving mill industry in the town and that one of the mills was then used to provide Ashford House and its fountains with water, and that, in making his improvements, he had pulled down some of the town houses. Much of what went on on large estates would have been organised by the land agent and at Ashford the improvements were carried out under the active superintendance of William Burke, whose mother was Mary Anne, sister of Arthur Guinness of Beaumont near Dublin. Burke had been able to speak Irish since a child, and his obituary notes:

'Being able to speak the Irish language from boyhood he was brought so much closer in touch with the peasantry, by whom he was sincerely beloved, and will be affectionately remembered'.

Important agents were usually either family members or related through marriage and William Burke was a younger son of the Burkes of Ballydugan. His father was a clergyman and he himself a barrister. When he resigned, *The Tuam Herald* reported that Lord Ardilaun's house in London was 'besieged with applicants asking the post and putting forward every qualification under the sun to recommend them to his approval'.

His successor was James Jackson whose father had been Dean of Armagh and a member of a Yorkshire gentry family.

Through his agent Sir Arthur was able to maintain good relations with his tenants. Ten landlords controlled nearly half of the total land of County Mayo and nine of them were absentees. Although Sir Arthur was not resident, the negative aspects associated with absentee landowners were not evident at Ashford as they were on other properties in Mayo. Sir Arthur took great trouble with his tenants on his annual visits. When he and his wife arrived in Cong they were usually met by the tenantry in Ballinrobe, and the young men would pull the carriage from there to Cong. They would be greeted with bonfires

The columns of a chimney piece at Ashford Castle, by Lady Ardilaun

Photograph of a gamekeeper holding woodcock and pheasants (c. 1900)

and a general address 'in which all the principal local dignitaries participated.'

Moran tells us that when Guinness returned from three months convalescing in France following a serious illness in 1877, he was provided with a rousing reception from his tenants who came out to meet him in the worst possible weather. Another proof of his special relationship with them was when he insisted that those who had the franchise should have a free vote in the 1872 Galway by-election.

This was in stark contrast with most of the other landowners in County Galway who tried to dictate to their tenants how they should vote. As a former Conservative MP and a landlord it would have been normal for him to exercise some influence but he did not, and on the polling day he accompanied his voters to Oughterard to vote. He also ensured that he had a good relationship with most of his Catholic tenants' priests, which was important in 19th century Ireland where the clergy could make certain that social order was preserved in their parishes.

Sir Arthur provided financial support for their churches and schools at Cross, Curraghnamorsa, and Clonbur. The clergy were consequently careful to keep a check on their parishioners to ensure that there were no anti-landlord acts of aggression.

The most interesting of these priests was Father Lavelle, who was sent as Parish Priest to Cong in 1869. He had gained a reputation for being a most uncompromising opponent of landlordism after his dealings with Lord Plunket and other landowners at Partry. Within two years of his arrival in Cong, Lavelle had become a regular visitor to Ashford House and had mellowed in his attitude towards Irish landlords. Gerard Moran writes:

'This can be attributed to Guinness's influence. Sir Arthur was responsible for providing him with a parochial house, Lavelle having to reside with one of his parishioners after his arrival in Cong. He also provided Lavelle with a 13-acre grazing farm at Caherduff in 1871, and it was widely believed that Sir Arthur had paid many of Lavelle's debts incurred in his litigation against the Partry landlords in 1869. It was thus not surprising that many Nationalists who had previously supported Lavelle were angry with his liaison with the Guinness family.'

One correspondent to *The Connaught Telegraph* in 1879 stated: 'Cong is changed and so is Father Lavelle. The soft hand of Lady Olive has worked wonders. How she must have winked at Sir Arthur when Father Lavelle was parading the poor tenants and instructing them as to how they were to cheer on that festive occasion, which was described by him in a local contemporary as "Tenants rejoicing at Ashford".'

There was, however, one point on which Sir Arthur was not prepared to concede and that was the wellbeing and safety of his game in preparation for the great driven woodcock and pheasant shoots each autumn and winter that were his pride and joy. Compared with a threat to people's livelihood, the eviction of human beings from their only home and their consequent emigration, this might seem an inconsequential matter.

However, Moran explains:

'Guinness was prepared to use the full rigours of the law against the people if they trespassed onto his property, in particular the woods and lakes which he stocked for fishing and shooting.'

He forbade the keeping of dogs without which, the tenants alleged, the rat population increased, reducing the amount of corn available. The setting of game traps was strictly forbidden, as was the cutting of heather on the hills which was used by the tenants for bedding for their cattle. In most cases they had to pay heavy fines—in April 1874 30 tenants were fined 2s.3d. each at Clonbur Petty Sessions for 'pulling heath at Coolin Mountain. The tenants argued that they required the heath for cooking purposes because of a scarcity of fuel.'

If there was one issue over which there was any bad feeling between landlord and tenant on the Ashford estate, then this was it.

Sir Arthur was a man of principle. His political views had remained the same ever since that letter written by his brother when they were both in their twenties. He could not and did not believe that it was better for Ireland to be independent of England and was not prepared to support the Nationalist sentiments that swept the country after 1874 under the guise of Home Rule. The influence of the Fenian organisation was particularly strong in the Land League movement in the Cong and Clonbur region at this time, which immediately put Sir Arthur in the opposite camp. Moran continues:

'The importance of collective action was such within the Land League, that it was imperative for the success of the agitation that everybody adhered to the same policy to ensure rent reductions were secured. While most of the Guinness tenants were in a position to pay their rents they were told to withhold them.'

This, of course, had a very bad effect on relations within the estate and, reading between the lines, one can see that Sir Arthur was extremely angry. He was furious at the Land League's threats and intimidation tactics. Hurt but stubbornly determined he decided that since the rents were not being paid he could not employ the usual number of artisans and labourers so that in 1879–80 only 100 were on the payroll compared with the usual 400 or 500.

Sir Arthur knew the plight of his tenants, but felt that he had been bullied and manipulated so unfairly that he refused to give in to their demands in the early months, although he softened in the end. In a letter to the *Galway Express* on 1 December, 1879, he sympathised with his 'Friends and Tenants' and gave them a little lecture about saving for a rainy day saying that he believed a panic was being artificially created and small farmers had allowed themselves to be seduced into debt that, with greater prudence, they might easily have avoided.

He was outraged by 'the abominable intimidation' that had been committed against the people who wanted to pay their rent and claimed that the people to whom they owed money were the ringleaders in an unjust and wicked agitation against the landlords. He warned them against political agitators, and argued that he would never give into threats. Those very threats had dissuaded him from offering help before now.

He wrote:

'Nothing shall ever induce me to yield one inch to such unworthy and disgraceful efforts to influence you and me, and create between us feelings of irritation and distrust which have never hitherto existed.'

He pointed out that he had spent more than double his rental each year on the property since succeeding to it and that his father before him had 'in the bad times, placed food and fuel within the reach of those unable to obtain them otherwise.'

Neither he nor father had ever raised the rents and he offered abatements: 'On all holdings under 20 pounds rent, 30 per cent; on all holdings from 20 to 50 pounds rent, 20 per cent.' Then came the icy shower:

'Excepting leaseholders and tenants in town holdings, and some tenants on my mountain estate who, in consequence of their conduct towards me, deserve no favours at my hands'.

This letter appeared on 5 December 1879, and on 13 December there was a report in the same paper of a large bonfire being lit in the village of Cong where the people and those of the surrounding district were determined to express their gratitude for his kindness and moves to see the poor of his property safely tided over the present crisis. When it was discovered that the Guinnesses were returning from a trip, the people met them and, taking the horses from the carriage, drew it themselves into the village.

'Sir Arthur briefly addressed the immense crowd … expressing a hope that no influence whatsoever would succeed in causing a moment's distrust between them.'

The Rev. Mr. Lavelle addressed the people at length and said he was 'unable to express his delight at the spontaneous expression of their gratitude to their good and benevolent landlord.'

Sir Arthur also included £3,000 for meal and seed potatoes, but sadly, even this generosity was overshadowed by his decision to exclude the tenants on his mountain pastures because of their opposition to him in the past. So, as Gerard Moran points out,

'Guinness was ensuring that those tenants who were loyal to him received total help, but those who caused him trouble would not be helped. As other landowners used the notice to quit to ensure their tenants behaved themselves, Guinness used the threat of the withdrawal of relief to keep them in check'

The Land League's attitude to his agent William Burke only exacerbated the difficulties on the estate. Burke was also agent for Lord Kilmaine and Lord Clanmorris and much of the ill-feeling towards Guinness during the Land League days can be attributed to Burke. Due to his eviction notices to tenants on the Clanmorris estate and his treatment of the Noonan family in Cong, he was one of over 100 people in Mayo who had to receive police protection by the end of 1880.

There were also various accusations levelled against Sir Arthur. One was from a parish priest Father Walter Conway of Clonbur, who had failed to secure money for repairs to his church, and one from the Noonan family, which turned out to be the result of a family squabble over a house that actually belonged to their uncle. Guinness was obliged to evict one part of the family in order to re-instate the other part, to whom the house actually belonged. This matter was ended by Bridget Noonan throwing a bucket of scalding water over the agent as he rode through Cong on 13 June, 'for which she was duly arrested and imprisoned'.

It must have been difficult for the leaders of the land agitation to discredit the Guinnesses, as Sir Arthur had always been portrayed as a caring and progressive landlord. Nevertheless, there were stresses and strains and Father Conway was bitter in his reproaches:

'I must for the present be content with saying that I have never witnessed such callous and heartless indifference to the moral and religious, as well as the social and physical, well-being of the people as I have since I came to this parish. If landlordism here is to be taken as a specimen of the institution I would say unhesitatingly, "Away with it — cut it down". Give them what they would not grant their unfortunate serfs, compensations, and let them no longer lumber and curse the sacred soil of Ireland. You have only to look around, and from the very platform on which you are standing you can see the swaying forests which have superseded the fields of waving corn which was prepared by those mills which have shared the fate of other sources of employment, and which are now razed to the earth, or standing idle and silent as the tomb.'

It was later found by the leading Land League newspaper in the West of Ireland *The Connaught Telegraph*, that Father Conway's allegations were totally without foundation.

Gerard Moran writes:

'As in other parts of Connaught the distress of 1879–80 had a devastating effect on the Cong region. By the second week of January 1880 there were over one thousand people in need of relief, and it reached its height in early April when 2,333, or 70 percent of the population around Ashford had to be aided. It necessitated the establishment of a relief committee in Cong in January which was chaired by Guinness. It included twenty of the most influential people in the parish, including Lavelle as secretary. Two factors were responsible for the high levels of distress in the region. There was a high proportion of labourers and tradesmen in the Cong area and the downturn in economic activity in the late 1870s brought great hardship. As we have seen only one-quarter to one-fifth of the labourers employed by Guinness were now given full employment. While Guinness attempted to aid his tenants by providing meal, there were eleven other estates in the parish whose owners did little or nothing to assist their tenants. The good relations that existed in Cong can be seen in the composition of the Cong Relief Committee, which included farmers, landowners,

*Tea and tennis at Ashford
Castle (c.1880)—Lady
Ardilaun is seated beside the
silver hot water kettle*

Picnics during a shoot at Ashford Castle—Lady Ardilaun wears a muff and her husband,
Lord Ardilaun, lies at her feet

doctors and clergymen of all persuasions. It was more representative in its composition than in most of the neighbouring parishes. There is little doubt that without Guinness' magnanimous help his tenants in Cong would have endured greater hardship than was the case. His involvement with the central committee of the Mansion House Relief Committee meant that more funds were made available to the Cong/Clonbur region than came from Land League sources. While the Mansion House Relief Committee expended less than one-tenth of this sum, the Cong Relief Committee received virtually nothing from the Land League. Two factors were responsible for this—the fact that Guinness and other landlords were involved on the committee made the League's leadership loath to forward funds to such local groups. At the same time there was Guinness' detestation of the League itself. The demise of the Land League after 1882 helped to partially restore the relationship between Guinness and his tenants in Cong. The annual addresses of the tenants to their landlord and the general festivities at Ashford Castle returned when he visited his estate. However, circumstances in the region had changed. The legacy of the Land League made the tenants more vocal in their demands for peasant proprietorship, and the emergence of the Home Rule issue made Guinness, or Lord Ardilaun, as he had become in 1880, aware that life would never be the same in Cong. As a result of this he was one of the first landlords in Mayo to sell off his estate to his tenants under the terms of the 1885 Ashbourne Land Act. While Guinness enjoyed a good rapport with his tenants he was determined to exercise a strong hand against those tenants who had the potential to cause trouble. He wanted an estate where all could share the benefits of his improvements. However, as with all such developments, there are winners and losers. In order to make the holdings more economical land had to be consolidated. Nevertheless Guinness' rule and its legacy must be seen in the light of the improved circumstances it brought to most of the people of his Western estates.'

From this detailed and clear-sighted survey it can be seen that the Land War was the cause of great anxiety and stress for a conscientious landlord with determined views, and that the aims of a productive estate and a contented tenantry were difficult to combine. The leaders of the land agitation were in the unusual position of discrediting a benevolent landlord. Nevertheless, the unpicking of the threads that were to progressively loosen through political agitation over the next 40 years had begun, and relations between landlord and tenant would never be the same again. In his wonderful book, *The Twilight of the Ascendancy* Mark Bence Jones recounts a story from 1880:

'Even from a mere twenty miles away, the special correspondent of *The Daily Telegraph* in the West of Ireland heard exaggerated reports of the plight of Lord Ardilaun, the former Sir Arthur Guinness, who had recently been raised to the peerage. He was said to be beleaguered at Ashford Castle, his life threatened on account of his alleged refusal to allow his tenants to cut turf on their own

hills and because he had lent some horses to his neighbour Captain Boycott. The correspondent braved a snowstorm in order to interview him, and on the way talked to the country people who all agreed that he was an exceptionally good and generous landlord, but kept on saying: "He's not liked, sir, he's not liked". At Ashford there was no sign of any siege. No soldiers or police guarded the gates, while inside the beautiful demesne labourers were peacefully at work brushing leaves from the paths. Lord Ardilaun seemed perfectly happy in his brand-new castle of gleaming cut-stone on the wooded shores of Lough Corrib, where his steam yacht lay at anchor. The correspondent asked him if he considered himself to be in any danger. "Well, no," he replied laconically, "Police have been offered me for my protection, but I have a little force of my own consisting of my gamekeepers, who are loyal men and true, and I prefer to trust to them. Besides, my tenants are all on good terms with me, even though they may be frightened by those who are about them. I do not intend to even ask them for their rent until next January. They could pay it very well now, but I certainly shall not press them. Whatever danger landlords are in is owing to the agitation which goes on around us."'

Later, the correspondent had the chance of talking to one of the local leaders of the Land League, who said.

'I consider that Lord Ardilaun would be perfectly safe if he was to walk about amongst his tenants, because he is a good man and much liked here; but his agent is disliked and it is he who is unpopular.'

This fascinating snippet is accompanied by a group photograph of tea and tennis party for the gentry at Ashford Castle in September 1880. Lord Ardilaun is wearing a bowler hat and what looks like a rather haunted expression. Lady Rosse from Birr Castle is in the middle of the back row and the rakish-looking Barnie FitzPatrick stands on the extreme right, handing another lady a cup of tea (Lady Ardilaun's silver teaset can be seen in the hall of the hotel today). The fountain plays in the background, and the ladies wear very becoming tightly buttoned bodices and long skirts. The two tennis-playing gentlemen wear white caps and heavy tweed suits and quite ferocious expressions. They are all sitting on the new, white stone steps. Some of the ladies are decidedly plain, while others are quite young and graceful. Again we are held in suspense at not knowing what happens next. Perhaps the situation seems poignant because they do not know they are the last generation of an almost vanished race. Many of their descendants would be killed in the World War I, and the remainder would move away. Their families would be scattered, and their houses either burnt or left as empty shells around the countryside.

When the historian Froude wrote that 'the whole set of them will be swept away' he was right. Of about 200 'big houses' within a radius of 30 miles not a single one remains. The landlords, for all their brave words, were definitely on the losing side of the Land War. Soon the tenants would own the land and paying, or failing to pay, the rent would cease to be the national preoccupation.

Chapter 9

George Moore at Ashford

T he views of another landlord have been recorded by the author George Moore, owner of Moore Hall in County Mayo, who stayed at Ashford Castle with the Ardilauns during the 1880s. Moore was a very reluctant landlord and foresaw the doom of his class.

He is also well known for his French-inspired novels and for being an early appreciator of Impressionist painting and one of Ireland's greatest literary figures of the late 19th and early 20th centuries. *Parnell and His Island* is such a rare book that I was allowed to read it only in the rare book room by the librarian at Trinity College, Dublin. After I had finished he reverently removed the book from my hands, refusing to allow me to copy it myself, but kindly returning some time later with the copied pages that I needed. I have included the passage, as it is so relevant to the content of this book.

'A few days after our return from the north-west, my host said, throwing a letter across the table: "This is from Lady Ardilaun, a neighbour of mine, asking us on a visit to Ashford." All who do not live more than ten or twelve miles apart are next-door neighbours in Ireland, and as the jolting car pursued its way along the interminable roads, my friend told me all he knew of the people we were going to stay with. Lord Ardilaun is a man of immense wealth. It is said he sold his share in the great brewery (Guinness' brewery) for a million of money. This money he has invested in different securities all over the world; his landed property, although large, is only a small part of his income; he is the only man in Ireland who is in a position to defy the Land League. Hence his unpopularity.

'Is he unpopular?'

'For the moment; and it is a shame that it should be so, for no man ever lived who behaved more generously to Ireland than he. Others may be accused of drawing money from Ireland, and spending it on the banks of the Thames and the Seine, but not he. When he was a member for Dublin, he bought Stephen's Green; it was then a savage waste; he spent thousands of pounds planting trees, making artificial water, and enclosing it, and presented it to the city. He bought the Rotunda, made it into a beautiful winter garden, where people might go of an evening, walk and listen to the band playing. At first everybody thought it delightful; but sooner or later, like everything else in Ireland, it was sneered at, and when the people finally refused to go near it, it was sold. Lord Ardilaun was then member for Dublin, and at the next general election he was beaten. And the same want of sympathy is shown to him at Ashford. Would you believe it, he is guarded by policemen in a place where he has spent thousands and thousands of pounds, where he has done more real good—that is to say, good in the sense of encouraging industry, good in the sense of relieving suffering—than perhaps any Irishman that ever lived? At the present moment I hear that his labour bill is over two hundred a week. Any other man who had been requited as he has been would have left the country long ago; but when people are naturally good, they go on being good in spite of all opposition.

"Then how do you account for his unpopularity?"

"First, his large fortune enabled him to successfully resist the Land League, secondly he is a Protestant, and thirdly he is a Conservative. In Ireland popularity is bought with hatred of England; if you are a Catholic so much the better—indeed it is a distinct advantage to be a Catholic, but the first of all things is to hate England."

'While speaking we grow gradually conscious of certain changes in the aspect of the country: it seems more orderly, and it wears an air of well-to-do-ness that we had not before observed. The rickety walls built out of loose round stones piled one on the top of the other have disappeared and are replaced by handsome stone and mortar walls; and the cottages of the peasants are less dirty, and here and there the landscape is marked by small cleanly-built slated houses. Upon questioning our driver we learn that we are now entering upon Lord Ardilaun's estate, and as the panting horse drags the car to the top of a high hill he says, "That's Lough Corrib, the largest lake but one in Ireland, thirty miles long by ten wide."

'And the view as it now appears over the verge of the long line of sloping green sward is full of an august and visionary beauty. Below us, falling in sweet inclining plain, a sea of green turf flows in and out of stone walls and occasional clumps of trees down to the rocky promontories, the reedy reaches and the long curved woods which sweep about the castle—such a castle as Gautier would have loved to describe—that Lord Ardilaun has built on this beautiful Irish land. There it stands on that green headland with the billows of a tideless sea,

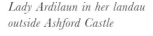

Lady Ardilaun in her landau
outside Ashford Castle

This view of Ashford Castle has changed dramatically, with the addition of the new wing around the old entrance

*An early view of the Castle
showing the old Browne
house on the right*

lashing about its base; and oh! the towers and battlements rising out of the bending foliage of ten thousand trees. The lake from where we stand looks like a girdle of pale grey silk bound about the green garments of the Emerald Isle: the long line of mountains upbreaking in jagged outlines, through a drift of clouds—now dark with storm, now resplendent with sunshine! And we lift unsatiated eyes from this rapture of scenical loveliness.

'We are still two miles from our destination and as we advance signs of wealth and industry increase. We pass large roads, domain walls in process of construction, and a large archway upon which at least a hundred men are at work. And as I gaze I ponder on the crookedness of the Celtic mind; it would put an end to all I see around me, and would willingly relapse into dirt and patriotism—which are apparently but two words for one and the same thing. On either side of us the park now spreads. Through the hillocks hundreds and hundreds of fallow deer move away at our approach, and over the crest of a hill the broad bluff red deer raise their antlered heads and gaze at us steadfastly as lions. From the deer-park we go into the drawing-room-like beauties of the pleasure-grounds, and

skirting by the laurel-filled nooks and rhododendron-covered slopes, overhung by the dark branches of cedars, we find ourselves facing the river, and it is only after some little difficulty that our horse is induced to trust himself on the picturesque wooden-way which in drawbridge fashion spans the inky stream which whirls round the point on its way to the lake.

'Those who love life welcome new impulses, and desire the emotion of unexpected impressions. I am such a one; and the simple pleasure of sitting at a farm window, watching the villagers strolling in bands and couples and single figures across the darkening green, listening to the chattering voices of loitering women, the howl of a distant dog, to all the vague sounds and shadows that mark the sinking to rest of the world, have never failed to thrill my heart with happiness. "The poetry of the wold is never dead", and to me it is now an exquisite delight as I stand in long shadowy saloon brushing my hair for dinner to see the moon shining on a vast lake, to watch the weird darkness of the buttresses and the romantic enchantment of the battlements, now standing out sharp against a silvery cloud, from which the moon slowly passes.

Connemara,
by Lady Ardilaun

Fishing on the Corrib

As Shelley would say,

> *'Like a dying lady, lean and pale,*
> *Who totters forth, wrapt in a gauzy veil,*
> *Out of her chamber, led by the insane*
> *And feeble wanderings of her fading brain.'*

'And after a week spent in the thin, mean poverty of the north-west, amid the sadness of ruined things, this strangely beautiful castle renders me singularly happy. The sight of the long drawing-room full of refined faces glowing upon the warm shadows, and the lights of the shaded lamps, comes with a sense of welcome relief. And to awake in the cool spaces of a bedroom, beautiful and bright with Indian curtains, and musical with the rippling sound of the lake's billow, is also full of gracious charm and delicate suggestion of poetry to him who is alive to the artistic requirements of today. And then there are the pleasant morning greetings to look forward to, and the sitting down to breakfast in the oak room within sight of the fountains that foam so lovely and so white upon an endless background of mountain and lake. Here we are almost shut out of the storm and gloom of crime and poverty that enfolds the land, but even here the shadow of murder and outrage falls across our way. For as we sit at breakfast we hear the smothered detonation of the dynamite exploding in the huge moat which our host is having cut through the solid rock, and sometimes small splinters of stone strike the windows. Fifty or sixty men are engaged upon this work; and, after breakfast, as we walk down the grounds, we examine this new fortification, when finished will separate the castle from the mainland. It is thirty feet deep by twenty feet wide.

"You see," says our host, "I have a taste for the picturesque. The moat will be protected by battlements, and canon will be placed at convenient distances. I shall be able to defend myself in case of invasion, and as the drawbridge will be raised nightly it will be difficult for the dynamiters to get at me."

'But the day I shall remember best of the four days passed in this beautiful western retreat is the last day. It has been arranged that we are to go in the yacht (she now rides at anchor, her steam up, under the castle walls) to picnic on an island some miles down the lake—an island famous for some late pagan and early Christian ruins. The day is breathless, but the sky is full of a soft grey light; and in the fairy-like silences of the lake, when nothing is heard between the pauses of the conversation but the ripple of the water along the vessel's side, and the subdued panting of the machine, the many aspects of this noble wilderness, the wild outlines of the guardian mountains, the dark promontories covered with rough wood, the marshy shores where the heron stalks, arise as supernaturally still and calm as the visions of an Icelandic god, and in the exquisite clarity every detail is visible; the shadows of the pines fall like ink into the smooth mirror.

'And now the chain rattles through the porthole, the steamer swings at anchor,

and we are helped by the sailors into the small boat. The island is a large one—some sixty or seventy acres—and on the side we landed on it is cultivated by three families, and the land has passed from father to son, so it is said, for the last thousand years. In any case the island has never been without its three families—there is the boat in which they transport their farm produce, there are their cottages, there is the graveyard, and here is the church that St. Patrick's brother (the hermit) built in the 5th century; and the paved path leading from it to his cell is distinctly visible along which he walked fourteen hundred years ago, and along which we walk today; and here are the pagan remains, but we cannot look further back. Behind this stone is the savage darkness out of which we, who now examine this mute record with gloved fingers slowly and painfully crawled.

'This little island is complete in itself—a little world lost and forgotten in the midst of a greater world. But lost though it be and forgotten, it is strangely present in our minds today, and the poetry it evokes is strongly intense and penetrating; and the nostalgia of the past holds me in tether, and I cannot escape it even when quaffing champagne on the tower built for picnicking purposes, nor when looking over Lady Ardilaun's shoulder while she sketches with a free and certain hand a long range of jagged mountains, one of the mountain prospects she loves so dearly, and with which her London drawing-room is so beautifully decorated. The scene is now supernaturally still. The day dies in pale greys and soft pink tints, and harmonies in mauve more delicate and elusive than the most beautiful Japanese water-colour; the lake hangs like a grey veil behind the dark pine-woods through which we wander making our way to the yacht; and at the vistas we look on the long wavy lines of mountains that enclose the horizon, and they seem now like women sleeping the sleep of enchantment, and the mountains whose precipitous bases rise out of the lake are as fabulous creatures in a northern legend guarding the solitude.

'Our eyes follow the black flight of the cormorant along the smooth greyness of the water and our souls are filled and stilled with a sadness that is at one with the knowledge that the dear day we have lived through is now a day that is over and done; and as we think of this lonely island, its ruined church, its grave-yard and the endless generations that lie there, we must dream of the lightness of life, of the oblivion that awaits us, of those eternal and simple truths of which even the centuries of barbarous dust lying beneath our feet has in its day dreamed of even as bitterly as we.

'On the following day I started for Dublin. The carriage is full of Irish Members and American agitators. They denounce the injustice of England, and proclaim the sweet Irish peace that will follow on Home Rule.'

George Moore, by Edouard Manet

Chapter 10

Edwardian Views

L ooking at the photograph of the group of
people enjoying tea at an Ashford tennis party,
we might begin to wonder what sort of life they
were leading in County Galway in the 19th
century. Patrick Melvin in his brilliant essay *Social Life of the
Gentry in County Galway* records the activities of this
vanished race and I quote him liberally throughout the
remainder of this chapter. Many of the gentry families
were Catholics who kept their European connections with
France and Italy from the days when their ancestors had
been forced to live or be educated abroad during the Penal
times in Ireland. Protestant families meanwhile often had
marriage and sporting links with England. Horses and
jockeys crossed and re-crossed the Irish Sea and religious
beliefs made no difference whatsoever to the common
bond of horse racing and hunting, which were the two
most passionate interests of the County Galway families.
Other manly sporting activities for the different seasons
included shooting, fishing, yachting, and cricket. Ladies
could join in the demon games of lawn tennis and croquet
that took place in the long summer afternoons between
neighbouring houses, as well as the regattas and theatricals
that always accompanied the Galway races.

At my home, Glin Castle, we have a silver salver
embossed with yachts and boats won by my husband's
ancestor the Knight of Glin in 1834 at the regatta in
Galway Bay during Galway race week. There were house
parties and calls to be paid, charitable enterprises to
support, agricultural shows, and county events to attend,
as well as foreign travel. Several houses had remarkable
libraries and cultivated travellers brought back works of
art from abroad. There were many more old families still

110

living on their estates than in any other part of the country and the most frequent form of social entertainment was the ball, of which there was an endless variety culminating with the most important of all, the Galway Blazers Annual Hunt Ball.

The grandees of the county carried on regardless, even though the lavish house parties and extravagant hospitality crippled the landlords of the more financially unsound estates. The Dillons of Clonbrock had estates of 28,000 acres all over the West of Ireland and could afford to lead their splendid sporting and society lives—yachting at Cowes for ten weeks and then returning to Galway in time for the Ballinasloe Horse Fair. When they had to cut back on expenditure during the Land War, it was agreed to dispense with the housekeeper, stillroom maid, nursery maid, second footman, valet, and to make do with a 'working butler'.

The 1st Marquis of Clanricard (1802–1874) of Portumna Castle was known as 'Jack the Devil', and was a true rake in the best tradition of Georgette Heyer. A leading figure in Paris and London, he hunted in

Yorkshire, loved gambling and card games, loved the theatre, caused several shocking scandals in his own county for holding drunken orgies and womanising, and was disapprovingly reported as having 'a fondness for low company'.

The 5th Lord Clanmorris sailed around the world, hunted in Australia and New Zealand, went racing in Gibraltar and pig-sticking in Morocco. While staying in Paris with the Duc de Stacpoole, 'he discovered that owing to an unlucky speculation he had lost his last available £2,000'. He still maintained an air of affluence by receiving woodcock from his Galway demesne every day at the Hotel Meurice!

What the upright and worthy Lord Ardilaun thought of his neighbour's history does not relate, but there is no question that the life lived in the big houses of County Galway, despite the worrying times, could be great fun.

Filson Young in *Ireland at the Crossroads* (1903) recounts the stories of 'the hard riding, hard drinking, hard dancing and deep sleeping' that went on 'in the simplicity and homeliness of those jovial days'.

Above and left, Welcoming scenes for The Prince of Wales visit to Cong and the Corrib in January 1905

Chapter 10

Lady Ardilaun and the Prince of Wales pose with the shooting party at Ashford

He tells of a dance being given in a house in Galway 'the seat of one of the oldest Galway families, noted for its hospitality'. Unfortunately, 'It was discovered that about twice as many people had been offered accommodation as the house could put up. But such a matter did not trouble the genial hosts. The dancing went on until 4 o'clock in the morning when the ladies all retired and filled the available beds in the house. There they slept in peace until 7 o'clock when they were awakened by the passage of the butler up and down the corridors, ringing a loud bell, and crying out, "Get up girls; the Boys wants the beds".'

In 1878 The Duke of Connaught, Queen Victoria's third son toured the province with which he was so especially connected. He hunted with the Galway Blazers, dined with the Bodkins of Annagh, and stayed with the Persses of Moyode. The following letter describing the Hunt Ball at which he was present was found in an envelope inscribed: *Description of Hunt Ball in Galway Feb. 1878.* Sir Arthur and Lady Olive Guinness were there, but

the atmospheric undercurrents about the "pecking-order" must have been considerable. It is written by Miss Eliza Redington to her sister, and gives us an irresistible *apperçue* of a Hunt Ball of that date:

'My dear Annie,

(to mention one name but this is for everybody).

You will expect a full account of the ball, and I find it hard to know where to begin to describe it. Arabella I know is going to send you her version, so all I can say will be tame to her story! We dined at Renmore, and were in the room an hour I'm sure before H.R.H. (Prince Arthur, Duke of Connaught) came: the time, however, was well spent in taking in and admiring all the arrangements. I had been told they had been "decorating the room" but was quite unprepared for what I saw. I could barely recognise the old room and passages and the well-known dark, dirty staircase. The place was transformed, just I should say, as when Cinderella's fairy turned the dirty kitchen into the ball room of the prince's palace! The hall and staircase

114

were covered in crimson cloth, the outer porch being decorated with flags, and the stair rails hung with festoons of crimson, most gracefully disposed, and looped up with bunches of pure white roses. Across the rail at the top of the stairs which faces the great landing was written in large letters of white roses on crimson *Welcome to Connaught*. Two more doors were made into the ballroom, one at each side of the centre door. In fact, it appeared as if all one room with 2 piers supporting the roof, where the wall and door used to be. The ballroom, supper room and refreshments rooms were all re-papered in pretty, rather artistic papers with dados.

'The windows had white lace curtains under hangings of crimson and gold, and between each window, and on opposite wall were very large shields of crimson cloth, with spurs, bits, hunting whips, foxes' brushes and stuffed heads most artistically arranged upon them to form designs; from time to time along the walls were smaller shields with a beautiful monogram of C.G.H. (County Galway Hunt) in gold upon them.

'Then the room was a blaze of light; and all from half coronas of wax candles which were placed along the walls in a continuous line all round. The passages, too, were well lighted with coronas and the main stairs with modorator lamps arranged between pots of leaf-plants (dracaenas, ferns, etc.) on the window-sills. The entire walls of the side lobbies (when one looks down below towards the refreshment-rooms, and whence the bed-rooms and side-passages go off), were covered with amber and white calico beautifully fluted on to the walls and forming broad vertical stripes of yellow and white; the floor and rails, even in these lobbies, being all crimson cloth.

'The entrance to the Duke's robing room was draped with crimson curtains edged with gold lace. Then all the side sitting-rooms were opened and lighted so that couples could sit out between the dances; and all the front of the hotel was illuminated with large stars of gas, so that the whole square was lighted up almost like the daylight. The refreshment-room and supper-room too were very tastefully arranged; plate, leaf-plants and flowers on the tables, which were well-filled; the eating, and drinking I thought very good.

'In fact, it was far away the most brilliant thing of the kind I have ever seen anywhere, and I am sure could scarcely be surpassed. You would not have known the place; and all would have been perfect if there could have been a few people less. Still it was not at all the crush I had been led to expect. (They say 300, I don't think it.)

'Not much dancing until supper-time, but always standing room. Everyone was well-dressed, too, and so many were there whom one does not often see at balls. Lizzie and Robert! She in black velvet and diamonds. The Guinnesses (she well dressed in orange and black), he very gracious (indeed both). Miss Trench of Woodlawn (very nice), and K. and G. Dillon (latter very nicely dressed, former not looking well) came from Lenaboy.

'From Glenarde Mrs and Miss Lindsay. Mr and Mrs A. Courtney and Edith Martin were staying in Galway,

The house party for the Prince of Wales—Lord Bandon (centre), the Prince of Wales (third from right), Lord Ardilaun (second from right), Percy La Touche (far right)

Lady Ardilaun entertains the local gentry

The village of Cong comes out to welcome the Prince of Wales

the Lairdners were there, (Miss looking so well). Emily Courtney (from Moyode, not looking very well in white). From Furbough, Lady Delvin, Lady Mary Burke (both beautifully dressed and Lady M. so nice,) Sir J. Burke and the Charlie Nugents. From Renmore Col. and Lady A.Daly (so well dressed and quite charming!) Miss Gascoyne (well got-up and piquant as usual), G. Martin, raggy but very pretty: and selves!!

'Then there were of course the ordinary people. Dalys, Blakes (any number of these), Lamberts (the "Brook-hill" girls did not look well), Helen Power, Frank Joyce, the Dolphins, Burkes of Ouer, etc. Arabella, Mr Algernon, and Gerald from Roxboro'. The Creg Clare party, you know.

'And now I come to the great failure of the night, the conduct of the Persses, which has raised the rightful indignation of the whole county and won't be forgotten for years! They kept the Duke as their own private preserve, and seem to have intended that he should dance with no one but their own family—"the great Persse Ring" C. calls it, (as they call the cliques and parties at New York) and I say the Ring should be called "the Duke of Connaught's Own".

'Lady O. Guinness went up to Mr B. P. (Burton Persse) (Georgie Dillon told me this and was indignant but don't quote her) and begged that the Dillons should be presented. Mrs B. P. brought up Capt. FitzGerald, and tried to pass him off on them, but Lady O. stood there and said the Duke should be presented to them (I think she knew him before) and then Mr. P. did it, but this was in the end of the night and he never asked them to dance.

'J. Lynch went to Mrs.B.P. and insisted that Lady A. Daly should be presented "she was his guest and he would not have her insulted" and it was done, but late in the

night, and he never danced with her nor I think was introduced or danced with her sister or Lady Delvin. I don't think Miss French was even presented! Fanny met him in the passage and was presented.

'I am sure Lizzie B. never was and he danced with E. Courtney (because she was staying at Moyode) and Miss Percy (that girl J. Blakeney wants to marry, the Lord knows why)!!! John Daly says the ladies and gentlemen at the ball made it pleasant, but he would not speak of the "inhabitants of kennels, that were not of course, human beings!!!" (Burton Persse was Master of the Galway Blazers).'

And so on for another page of gossip. Jane Austen and Mrs. Gaskell combined could hardly have risen to the same pitch of excitement at the despicable behaviour of the 'Persse Ring' in keeping the Royal personage to themselves. Harry Worcester Smith, an American who was a fanatical Master of Hounds in Ireland in 1912/13 recorded a visit to the Persse house at Moyode Castle, giving a long description of the former splendours of the deserted building, the park, gardens, and above all the magnificent kennels.

'Burton Persse was a keen old man and played the game to the limit. When times became bad in Ireland he went to Lord Ardilaun and mortgaged all his acres. When he died, as the heirs were not able to pay the mortgage, the place became the property of Lord Ardilaun, but the old sportsman had "lived" during his stay.'

Another and even grander Royal visit took place at Ashford Castle in 1905 and by this time 'Lady O. Guinness' had become Lady Ardilaun, and there was going to be absolutely no nonsense this time about not being introduced.

Lough Corrib was lit up by a fleet of steamers and sailing craft to welcome the Prince of Wales to Ashford

In fact, except for herself, the famous woodcock shoot was to be a men-only affair.

Gentry families in Connemara like the Martins of Ross were prevented from becoming followers of the Galway Hunt by the River Corrib, except when invited to a meet or hunt breakfast and had to be content with fishing, and snipe shooting. Shooting parties were especially popular in the 1850s and 1860s. These took place on the greater estates such as Clonbrock, Castle Hackett, Marble Hill, Dunsandle, Lough Cutra, Monivea, and Roxburgh. It was considered that :

' Lord Ardilaun had the best woodcock shoot at Ashford through careful preservation and judicious thinning and planting. He held a select shooting party at the end of every January'.

The great event was exhaustively reported in the papers and every detail has been recorded in the *Court Circular, The Irish Field, Vanity Fair, The Times,* the *Irish Times, Westminster Gazette, Madame,* and many others from which I have culled the following extracts. The house party included Lord Bandon, Lord Rathmore,

Colonel Robert Dillon (son of Lord Clonbrock), Major Acland Hood, and Mr. Percy la Touche from Harristown, Co. Kildare.

The *Court Circular* of 28 January 1905 reported:

'The Prince of Wales crossed from Holyhead on the Royal Mail steamer *Ulster*, and was met at Kingstown by the Lord Lieutenant, and landing soon afterward was driven by carriage to Dublin Castle for breakfast. He then proceeded to Broadstone station around 12 noon and caught the special train to Ashford. As he was in a private capacity no formalities were observed.

'At Ballinrobe, the nearest station to Ashford, he was received by Lord Ardilaun, Colonel Knox, the Archdeacon of Tuam, and Colonel Maurice Blake. The guard of honour of the Royal Irish Constabulary was mounted at the station, and he drove off to hearty cheers from the large number of spectators.

'The approach to Ashford Castle had been decorated with triumphal arches bearing the legends *Céad Míle Fáilte* and *God Bless the Prince of Wales* and the arrival of the Royal guest was the signal for a demonstration that partook of

The departure of the Prince of Wales attracts several interested onlookers

*Lady Ardilaun and guests on
the steps at Ashford Castle*

The Eglinton prepares for a cruise down the Corrib

the nature of a Highland greeting in the olden time.
A ghillie stationed on a neighbouring height whistled
shrilly when the Prince, accompanied by Lord Ardilaun
and Sir Charles Cust, drove in sight, and as soon as
he carriage was observed to gain the crest of the hill,
two rockets were sent up, accompanied by the
simultaneous illumination of the castellated gateway to
the demesne.

'Guns were also set booming from both far and near,
and a mighty shout of *Long Live the Prince of Wales* was
uttered by the assembled crowd. A double line of torch
bearers lined the avenue for some distance who as soon as
the carriage passed the gates, closed in behind and around
it, acting as guides for the half mile through the Deer Park
leading to the house.

'When this was reached the Prince gained a delightful
view of Lough Corrib and the fountain, lit up in the
dusk by a fleet of steamers and sailing craft, all burning
magnesium light in emulation of the fifty torches whose
bearers had marched round to the Lake Front.

His Royal Highness came to one of the windows,
where he stood for some time with his hostess, a pleased
spectator of the unfamiliar and beautiful scene.'

The Westminster Gazette of 31 January reported:

'The next day, Wednesday, was the first shoot early in the morning which was very satisfactory though the bag did not come within thirty of the record established at Ashford a couple of years ago when 211 woodcock were killed. By half past 8 the guns were on their way to Clonbur covert, a mile from the house, where shooting began at once with about 50 beaters driving the birds out into the open glades.'

'The Prince was in great form and shot magnificently, only one of the party exceeding by a solitary bird His Royal Highness's first day's record. Lunch was served in the Lunch House at Ballycoyne and the sportsmen shot on until dark, the day's count including 180 woodcock and a few pheasants. The shooting on Thursday was over the Ross Hill estate which skirts Lough Mask, and on two of the islands on the Lough—the smallest of which covers 150 acres.

'Glorious sunshine prevailed each day which was most disappointing for the host as hard frost is what is so essential for woodcock shooting. The bag on the concluding days of the week seldom held more than from 90 to 100 woodcock but a number of pheasants, partridges, and other birds were also shot.'

The other papers reported in almost identical terms:

'On Friday morning, the Prince drove through the village of Cong on his way to the Cong Rock coverts, and had an extraordinarily enthusiastic reception from the people who had put up the most wonderful decorations in his honour.

'Lord and Lady Ardilaun drove with his Royal Highness through the little town, but Lady Ardilaun returned to the house before the shooting began. She is in no sense of the word a sportswoman, and seldom joined the guns even at lunch. She is a sweet retiring woman with a charming face.

'A few outside guests came to dinner on several nights; otherwise the party spent a quiet evening at Bridge, and retired early after the fatigues of the day. Lady Ardilaun wore some lovely dinner gowns during the week, that on the evening of the Prince's arrival being especially beautiful, of white crepe de chine, trimmed with bands of ostrich feathers, the bodice draped with a fichu of exquisite old Irish point.'

'Lord Ardilaun did everything in Princely fashion during the week and forgot nothing which could add to his Royal guest's comfort and pleasure. The Prince must have found it hard to realise that he was in far off Connemara, that odd, wild corner of the earth which is supposed to have escaped the wand of civilisation.

Yet even there electricity has learnt to outstrip the sun his daily round, and the Prince, returning each evening from shooting was able to learn exactly what had happened that morning in St.Petersburg, since the thoughtful host had made special telegraphic arrangements for the convenience of his distinguished guest. His Royal Highness leaves today for Dublin where he will have a tremendously gay week at the Castle.'

And we know from another newspaper that:

'Lord and Lady Dudley the Viceroy and Vicereine invited a brilliant and "typically Irish" house party in honour of the Royal guest. His Royal Highness would take part in many brilliant gatherings including a Levee, and Drawing-room, and an Investiture of the Order of St. Patrick.'

In the memorabilia room at Ashford Castle today there is a framed letter from the Prince's private secretary, the future prime minister Neville Chamberlain, to Lord Ardilaun promising to keep security for the Prince well out of the way of the shooting:

'You may rely on the Royal Irish Constabulary keeping a vigilant eye 'outside' the coverts'.

In total, 444 birds were killed at the shoot for the Prince in 1905, while in 1910 the number went into the *Guinness Book of Records*—7 guns shot 587 woodcock. The Prince was delighted with his visit and Neville Chamberlain wrote a charming letter saying how much he had enjoyed himself. The heavily lidded Saxe-Coburg eyes of the future King George V gaze out benevolently from under his bristlingly tweeded cap at the centre of many a sporting group in photographs of the occasion.

Peter Campbell talks of the visit as if it was the other day. 'There were record bags,' he recounts with relish. 'A lot of Lords and Brigadiers of the time came to stay. Lord Bandon shot 44 woodcock with any amount of "rights and lefts" and twisters.' (The woodcock is known for being notoriously hard to hit as it twists and turns in its flight). On the day of the shoot Lord Ardilaun was noticeably tense and not his usual calm, collected self. He was not quite sure how the drives would develop and it was only as it became clear that everything was going to go smoothly that he was able to relax.'

Apart from the successful flushing out of the woodcock there could well have been other anxieties for the anxious host. Alexander Innes Shand, a self-confident young Scot described Ashford in his book *Letters From the West of Ireland* (1884):

'Ashford Castle is a noble pile of buildings in castellated style, partly of white granite, partly of grey limestone. Here again, as at Kylemore, vast sums must have been expended, and the neighbourhood far and near must have benefited by those golden showers. Nor has any one of the Ardilaun tenants, so far as I know, had cause to complain that his landlord has dealt hardly with him.

'Yet, on reliable information, precautions were taken for against Ashford being blown up by American dynamiters (Fenians) ... when he (Lord Ardilaun) entertained the gentry of the county at a ball, revolvers were *de rigeur* as a part of the ball costume, although they were left in the cloakroom with the hats and the overcoats.'

Perhaps as the host to the heir to the British throne Lord Ardilaun had more reasons than one to relax at the end of the Prince's peaceful visit!

Glorious Gardens

Andrew Campbell, later Lady Ardilaun's Head Gardener, was still 'a boy in the Bothy' in the early 1870s and learning his skills in the garden at St. Annes, Clontarf, when the 18-year-old Oscar Wilde came for lunch at Ashford Castle in 1872, shortly after the Ardilauns were married.

Oscar would have travelled from nearby Moytura, Sir William and Lady Wilde's (his parents) fishing lodge. Lady Ardilaun recounted the story of what happened when they stepped outside to look at the recently completed gardens, which must have contained massive amounts of bedding plants. Her cousin and companion Kathleen Everett retells the story in *Bricks and Flowers*, 1949 Thinking that her young guest might feel shy, Lady Ardilaun turned to ask him:

'Do you like my garden?'

'No,' he said clearly, 'it is very dull.'

Quite taken aback, Lady Ardilaun exclaimed, 'What do you mean?'

'I mean that it is very dull. Don't you think so'

'Don't you think my initials are well done?'

'Yes, but I don't care for them done in bedding plants, even if they are your initials'.

'The gardener wanted to do the family crest but as it's a pig, I wouldn't let him.'

'Oh, you should have. It would have been the perfect culmination of absurdity,' Oscar replied.

Kathleen recounts how Oscar got quite excited imagining how the picture could be done, suggesting flesh-coloured begonias for the body, and a houseleek, round and prickly, for the eye, and love-lies-bleeding pegged down in twiddles for the tail.

Olive Ardilaun always attributed her later profound interest in gardening to the shock she received from the youthful critic, and retained a real affection for Oscar all his life.

Lord Ardilaun's statue in St. Stephen's Green is the only official memorial left today to his many good works, but it is sometimes forgotten that in everything he did he was supported by his gentle, serene wife who adored him. They made a handsome pair, and she was to stand with ramrod-straight back beside him all his married life. Her own charitable impulses went hand-in-hand with his, and after his death she was well known for her many kindnesses to those in need.

Sensitive to the feelings of others, capable and persistent, she would have liked to work herself, but with the forbearance of the aristocratic Victorian wife of a proud and wealthy man, she accepted that could never happen. She was always sheltered and the hierarchical nature of her household and gardens was carefully constructed so that she would not have to raise a finger.

Left, The new spring leaves on the weeping willows Below, Flower beds and beech trees in winter on the Terrace Walk centred on the fountain in a very early photograph

'I should have enjoyed doing some actual work,' she confided to her cousin Kathleen Everett, 'but it wasn't possible. Once I pulled up a weed or two, but my dear old Head met me in the very act and looked very pained and hurt, and the next day there were men and boys in every border and by-way hunting stray weeds like sleuth-hounds.'

The tradition of making gardens was in her family and her grandfather, the 2nd Earl of Bantry, filled with longing to emulate the gardens of Italy on his return from the Grand Tour, had laboured for many years employing hundreds of people up to the last years of the famine, in making the beautiful setting for Bantry House.

Olive Ardilaun had a great deal of theoretical knowledge, and with her husband's help and that of her famous head gardener, Andrew Campbell, planned and planted two enormous gardens, one at St. Annes, Clontarf, now a much visited public park, and one at Ashford Castle.

She started to make another at Glengarriff Castle near Bantry but later gave it up, which must have been when her husband had bailed out her family from their

A basket of flowers from the garden

many financial embarrassments. Her greatest resource all her life were her flowers and her gardens. At Ashford she and her husband planned the Terrace and the Broad Walks—great sweeping vistas lined with trees, with areas of bedding plants picked out in shaped beds. Andrew Campbell was a specialist in the raising of several different herbaceous lobelias and *Lobelia Lord Ardilaun* was a soft scarlet with reddish leaves. The magazine *Irish Gardening* (Vol III, 1912) describes the garden at St. Annes:

'The large oval beds each containing several hundred plants of one variety, give quite a mass of colour'.

It is most likely that the bedding-out would have been the same at Ashford and there is a suspicion that the perennial herbaceous *Lobelia Eulalia Berridge* just might be a unique survivor from some of the plants grown there by Andrew Campbell. In the *Journal of the Irish Garden Plant Society* (Vol. 8) Dr. Charles Nelson writes:

'Among the *Lobelia* cultivars that Andrew Campbell raised at St. Annes were *Gloire de St. Annes*, *Lord Ardilaun*, *Morning Glow*, *The Bishop* and *Firefly*—they are *Lobelia syphilitica* hybrids involving *L. cardinalis* and perhaps other species. The proximity of Ashford Castle (at Cong) which was also owned by Lord Ardilaun, and Ballynahinch, Connemara (where the plant was known to have come from), seems to point towards this possible history, but there is no sufficient description that could indubitably link it to any of the Ardilaun plants. The only matter that can be stated with certainty is that *Lobelia Eulalia Berridge* has been cultivated in Ireland since the 1930s at least and nothing resembling it was known, at least to Graham Stuart Thomas, among the herbaceous *Lobelia* cultivars grown in Britain.'

Dr. Nelson tells us in his book *An Irish Flower Garden* that another beautiful plant propagated by Andrew Campbell from a sport of the old Bourbon rose *Souvenir de La Malmaison* was a 'charming rose' named by Lady Ardilaun herself as *Souvenir de St. Annes*. The rose was jealously protected. Lady Ardilaun would not generally give the new rose to other gardeners, but the odd cutting was passed to trusted friends after they had solemnly promised to let no-one else have it.

The rose did not become commonplace. Luckily, the famous gardener Lady Moore, widow of Sir Frederick Moore, the director of the Botanic Gardens in Glasnevin for many years, preserved it in her garden at Willbrook House, Rathfarnham.

A long time after her friend Lady Ardilaun's death, Lady Moore finally succumbed and gave the rose to Graham Stuart Thomas who propagated it and made it more widely available commercially in the early 1950s. Today it flourishes in many Irish gardens—the sculptured deep pink buds and shell pink flowers with yellow stamens bloom from late May, remaining constantly in flower to the autumn with a fragrant scent, few thorns, and fine dark green leaves.

There were various opinions about the garden at St. Annes. According to Dr. Nelson a visitor wrote in 1884 that it possessed:

*The fountain and its pool
was one of Lady Ardilaun's
innovations—her mother,
the old Countess of Bantry,
stands at the front of
the group*

'the greatest charm for the real lover of good gardening … I can conscientiously say that the herbaceous borders at St. Anne's are by far the neatest and best kept I have ever seen.'

However, he reports that the excellent if critical English gardener, Miss Ellen Willmott 'met Lord and Lady Ardilaun in France and commented in a letter to Frederick Moore that she 'was surprised how very little (Lady Ardilaun) knew about plants and gardening, in fact no more than she had known six years ago, but she told me her garden at St. Annes was quite wonderful and that she had worked it up until it was quite first rate in every way,' Miss Willmott remarked that she had heard such different opinions about St. Anne's that she was confused, adding "whatever be the case it is most fortunate that the owner is so completely satisfied".'

Which must be the firmest 'put-down' given to any garden owner to date!

The Ardilaun's houses were always full of flowers, and Andrew Campbell outlines his thoughts on growing them in several gardening periodicals such as *Irish Gardening*. In spite of being a modest and retiring man, so much so that his merits were sometimes overlooked—he was deeply respected in his profession and well known to almost everyone connected with gardening.

A walk round the garden with him soon revealed the depth of his knowledge and the extreme accuracy of his observations and deductions. He was much in demand as a lecturer and was always encouraging to young gardeners.

In her obituary of him in *Irish Gardening* (Vol XIII) in 1918 Lady Ardilaun wrote:

' He rose to be foreman, and, after some years, went to my cousin Harry Herbert of Muckross, and to the Railway Hotel at Killarney as Head Gardener. In these two places he remained for six years and then came to us at Ashford as Head Gardener where he was for 14 years and returned to St. Annes in 1895, so that he was with us for the whole of his working life. Forty-eight years with the exception of the six years he was at Killarney. He helped me to lay out the whole of the Pergola Garden at St. Annes interpreting every wish I ever expressed and every plan I ever formed. I do not remember ever having a disagreeable word with him all the years we worked together. He was the most loyal and devoted friend.'

He had great success with the growing of fruit, and of such varied plants as cyclamen, carnations, orchids, pot violets, alpines, roses, and herbaceous plants of all kinds,

'A feat which cannot be accomplished by any ordinary man', his obituary continued.

There is a sunken walled garden at Ashford where Andrew Campbell grew the vegetables and cutting flowers for the castle and raised his prize-winning lobelias and Japanese anemones. In a report written for *The Garden* in October 1892 he explained how he had:

'Observed a head of seed on a plant of *Anemone japonica alba*. This I sowed when ripe and got three seedlings from it. One of these I found much finer than the other two. From this plant the stock has been raised.'

An early photograph of the old gatehouse, which is now incorporated into the new wing of the hotel

Calling it *Lady Ardilaun* he gave it to Messrs. Lemoine who obtained a series of seedlings exhibiting 'the greatest diversity of variation in habit, size of flower, doubleness, and also in colouring'

The white *Beauté Parfaite* and the pink *Rosea Superba* were put on the market in 1894 and in a few years there were more than 30 Japanese anemones in the group all springing from the same seedling. The magnificent gardens at St. Annes and at Ashford and the plants Andrew Campbell propagated there were his worthy memorials.

I think that besides gardening Lady Ardilaun's other great interest was genealogy. She had a very clear idea of who she was and was fascinated by the family history of her own family, the Whites, Earls of Bantry of Bantry House overlooking Bantry Bay. She also loved her own family home Macroom Castle, County Cork, where, as the daughter of the younger brother of the Earl, known as 'Billy Hawthorne', she had grown up. When Macroom Castle was burnt by the IRA during the War of Independence she was heart sick:

'It was my trust to guard and care for. It withstood Cromwell's siege and has seen plenty of trouble ever since. My dear, dear home.' she moaned, as she walked from room to room when she was a widow living alone in St. Annes. At one point when Muckross, her mother's family home on the lakes of Killarney, was threatened by a sale, Lord Ardilaun generously stepped in and bought it for her to save it from 'commercial interests'.

Lady Ardilaun adored Ireland, and felt that she was Irish to her very bones. A superb hostess she presided over the dinners and balls that the Ardilauns gave in Dublin, in Ashford Castle, and in their huge house at Carlton House Terrace, in London. As her husband was an MP for many years, politics would have played a large part in their lives in Westminster, but at the same time I think her real satisfaction with life and her connection with people took place in Ireland. I believe that she led a shielded life, and might have liked to have led a slightly less stately one, but I have been unable to locate any of her own diaries or letters that could have led me to a greater understanding of her character. I have, therefore, had to rely on contemporary reports from friends who knew her, such as Lady Gregory in her journals, or on the stories of her cousin Kathleen Everett in her own autobiography *Bricks and Flowers*.

For many years Olive Ardilaun must have led an untroubled existence apart from her anxieties about her feckless brother. She would have been a leading member of society, taking part in the social and charitable life of Counties Galway and Mayo and also of Dublin and London, and vying with her sister-in-law, Lady Iveagh, in the splendour and magnificence of the parties and balls that they both gave. At Ashford Castle there are sepia photographs of Victorian and Edwardian garden parties with ladies in hats, long dresses and gloves, and gentlemen in top hats strolling rather self-consciously in the gardens by the water. In the evenings there would have been dances in the Castle hall with musicians playing in the gallery.

Autumn colour in the garden

Mowing the lawns at Ashford Castle—the dray horses wear special leather shoes to avoid marking the lawn

On the death of her husband she felt shattered and abandoned and was sure that her life had come to an end, and, although she inherited three houses, she chose to live exclusively in St. Annes at Clontarf.

When Kathleen Everett visited her cousin two years after Lord Ardilaun's death, she found her living alone at St. Anne's, where the wind whistled through the decayed and leaking 'Winter Garden' in the beautiful Turner conservatory. The Ardilauns had transformed the house from the original villa into, in the words of Lady Gregory, 'a portentous and pretentious' vast neo-Palladian palace that was freezing indoors.

'The dark enormous hall was intersected midway by a wide, cold, white marble staircase,' Kathleen Everett remembers, and thinks of her cousin as she saw her then, a tall, slight, black figure flitting across the cavernous hall, a lonely widow living alone in what felt like a mausoleum. Kathleen persuaded her to join the two small 18th century brick houses that she owned in St. Stephen's Green. Together they made a charming town house (number 42) and this dolls' house gave her more pleasure than all of her other mansions put together.

She held afternoon parties in the drawing room and presided over a sort of salon in 1917 where the unlikely and different circles of Dubliners during that turbulent time met for cups of tea. W. B. Yeats recited his poetry there and there were musical recitals from time to time. Lady Ardilaun's sympathy and affectionate interest as well as her unassailable position in society, seems to have touched and flattered people of very conflicting views— Douglas Hyde, George William Russell (A. E.), James Stephens, W. B. Yeats, Dublin lawyers doctors and professors, Lady Gregory and country friends, English soldiers and officials from the Castle and Garrison as well as 'outstanding figures in the Sinn Fein movement' to name but a few. Her cousin in *Bricks and Flowers* rather ambiguously underlines the fact that they were opposed to the nationalist movement, feeling horror at the murders of British soldiers and Irish policeman, and so were 'not' friends with any of the 'fanatical leaders'. As the widow of an extreme Unionist it would have been considered most unsuitable for Olive Ardilaun to have been entertaining any members of Sinn Fein at all!

She remained, however, an upright figure of the *ancien regime* and felt that the old world was falling to pieces around her. She loved the theatre, and was a great friend of Lady Gregory, helping her to support the Abbey Theatre in its hour of greatest need. Elizabeth Coxhead in her book *Lady Gregory* (1961) records that:

'Lady Ardilaun, the good friend who had tided them through other crises sent a cheque for £500. The Abbey was safe for the moment.'

Lady Gregory writes in her journals for November 1924 that she goes to tea with Lady Ardilaun in 'her bright flower-filled house'. The next day Lady Ardilaun brings a party to the Abbey Theatre and carries off Lady Gregory to tea at St. Stephens Green. Lady Gregory compares the experience to acting in two different plays—one in a world

Rhododendrons in spring

that is so alive at the Abbey, and the other so in decay. She describes the tea party as:

'a lament for banished society. The Bishop's wife talked of the burned houses and if they rebuild them they will be burned again. And if they are not burned who will want to live in them with no society? And all we are paying in postage! And the posts so slow in coming ... Lady Ardilaun herself, very good and bright, loving our Theatre and gathering what scraps of surviving friends she can, yet angry with the people—"all bad". But in practice she is kind and if she lived in the country I am sure would help them. She says there is no chance of any young man of our class getting employment in the future.'

Lady Gregory records in her own daily journal:

'An afternoon with Lady Ardilaun at St. Annes. She will give help to the Abbey if we need it. She is a lonely figure in her wealth—childless and feeling the old life shattered around her. She laments for Ashford, now a Barrack, and for the loss of Society and 'those nice young officers who used to write their names in our book' and she speaks with violent despair over Government and its opponents—"our class is gone and who is there to replace it?" She is *grande dame* all through, and her welcome touched me, she took my hands and kissed me. Her lovely garden is, she says, the one thing that keeps her there.'

Kathleen Everett tells the story of when her cousin was visiting some poor friends in hospital around the time that Sinn Féin was stealing cars. Looking out of the window Lady Ardilaun wondered aloud what would happen if they had taken hers. An old man in a nearby bed whom she had loaded with tobacco, cakes and sweets, said eagerly:

'But, my lady, the tram passes your gate.'

'I've never been in a tram.'

This statement caused a sensation, and the words, 'Never been in a tram' were murmured from bed to bed.

'Nor in a bus,' she added.

Then she sat down and told them how, when she travelled to London, the head coachman would always leave three or four days before she did with a carriage and a pair of horses and a groom. The second coachman would drive her to the ferry, where she was met by her agent who would take her down to the cabins engaged for her and her maid, already filled with flowers from her own garden. The footman who had been in the carriage to the ferry would travel on the same boat so that when they arrived at Holyhead he was there to look after them and take them to their reserved carriage on the train. At each stop he would come to the window to see whether there was anything else they needed. When they arrived at Euston Station her coachman, 'dear old Horton' was waiting to meet her with her own carriage.

'It was pure fairy story to the eager listeners,' says Kathleen Everett and it is a fairy story to us today. Her audience then wanted to know whether she had met Queen Victoria.

'Yes, of course, often in London. But the old Queen didn't treat Ireland too well. When she was young she and the Prince Consort came to stay with my mother's people at Muckross, in the south, and about fifty years later she came again and paid me an afternoon visit.'

'Did you give her a cup of tea?' they asked eagerly.

'Yes,' she laughed 'and a bunch of flowers'.

'And she'd like a cup of tea as well as any old woman, wouldn't she?'

She also told them about her visits to Buckingham Palace and described 'the splendour and tradition of an Abbey coronation'.

With 'her real Irish gift for description' she brought the whole scene to life for the sick patients, who listened, so we are told, 'without a trace of envy'.

Olive Ardilaun helped many old people as well as young, including a home for retired governesses, a vagrant's shelter, hospitals, churches, and schools. At Alexandra College, the famous Dublin girls' school, she endowed the Ardilaun Scholarship for Horticulture and

A splash of red on a spring day

eminent professors gave the annual Ardilaun Lecture. A former pupil, the late Mrs. Moira Reid was a native of County Clare and a gardener all her life. As a girl she won the Ardilaun Scholarship prize regularly and remembered being taken to tea with Lady Ardilaun at St. Annes nearly every year by her proud headmistress at Alexandra, Miss Henrietta White.

Miss White, along with Miss Fanny Currey of Lismore were the two ladies who in 1896 had persuaded—almost by force—Sir Frederick Moore, to institute a training course for women at the Botanic Gardens, where he was Keeper. Dr. Nelson tells us in his book *An Irish Flower Garden* that these two ladies belonged to a circle of eminent gardening women that included the Duchess of Leinster and Lady Ardilaun.

Another time, some workmen whom Kathleen Everett remembered as being repatriated prisoners of war came for the afternoon to see the house and gardens at St. Annes. Lady Ardilaun saw that her butler, Millions, (that was his real name!) took trouble with the tea and used the best china cups and displayed plenty of flowers.

Fifty men came to tea. She sat at one table and her cousin at another and the tables were loaded with wafer-thin bread and butter, butterfly-sized sandwiches and sugar-coated petits fours cakes Her cousin writes in *Bricks and Flowers*:

An early view of the formal gardens at Ashford (c.1880)

'Don't you think,' I ventured, 'they would be happier in the servants' hall with more substantial food?'

'No,' she answered, 'They are going to have our sort of tea with us, and the servants to pour it out and hand cream and sugar, and the best china is to be used'.

'How right she was! For as we stood in the portico to say goodbye, an ex-sergeant stepped forward, saying in a loud, ringing voice, "My lady, I speak for all present, for every one of us wants to tell you what you have done for us to-day. You have sat down with us, you have eaten with us, and all your servants have waited on us, and we feel you have wiped out the shame of having been spitted on in the streets of Berlin when we were handcuffed prisoners. My lady, we thank you with all our hearts." He stepped back his face quite crimson.

'Weren't they touching?' Olive said when we were alone. 'And you need not worry about their not eating much at tea because I have arranged for them all to have a good, solid dinner directly they get back to Dublin.'

Kathleen Everett remembers the story of a quick-witted old lady to whom a doctor's wife complained that Lady Ardilaun's garden parties were 'very mixed socially'

'Yes, she does mix her parties,' the old lady agreed dryly, 'I was asked to meet Queen Victoria.'

Soon after her husband died in 1915 Lady Ardilaun erected an obelisk on the Corrib shore to his memory in

*Dappled sunlight in
the garden*

a place that they had often escaped to be together and where she would go to sketch and paint. The inscription *Rien ne m'est plus, Plus ne m'est rien* is hewn into the granite and one feels it must have exactly described her feelings of absolute desolation.

Peter Campbell says that the obelisk is seven metres tall, weighs ten tons, and that over 120 people were employed to give a helping hand when it was erected. Lady Ardilaun could not bear to go to Ashford very often once her husband was gone, and indeed a codicil in his Will (dated 25 February 1902) bequeaths Ashford, Cong, Strand Hill, Lislaughy, Ross Hill and Doon estates to his brother Viscount Iveagh 'absolutely believing him the best person to deal with them, as it would impose too much care on my darling wife'

His wife was to live on in Dublin, although lonely and heartbroken. Again Lady Gregory remembers a visit to Lady Ardilaun's garden at St. Annes in 1923/4:

'Even now a wonderful display of flowers, dahlias chiefly, and roses. She finds solace in kindness, showed me in a glasshouse a quantity of geraniums in pots that are grown for poor women of the tenement houses who come to tea sometimes. She gives them a pot each to take away. She entertains patients from the Incurables Hospital and has a Charlie Chaplin film put on for them, gives the nearly blind rector's wife a wireless, and is tremendously interested in all Lady Gregory's theatre activities and her Players.'

By 25 December 1925 Lady Ardilaun is dead and Lady Gregory remembers:

'She was so good to the Abbey, so full of interest in it. And to the end so handsome, so erect, still keeping some of

*An albino woodcock shot at
Ashford in the 1930s*

the beauty I remember long ago. One day she came over (to Coole) from Lough Cutra and I gave her some scarlet cactus dahlias, then a novelty, and she held them to her face as she walked. She, Mrs. Jack Gardner, Enid Layard, Duchess Adeline, great ladies, in the first rank of any I have known.'

In the autumn today at Ashford Castle the yellow and golden leaves tell the story of the planting. Small stone mock-Gothic look-outs guard an enclosed space with a laurel hedge. Bay trees stand in squares of boxwood and everywhere maples are a brilliant crimson. The great stone pool and fountain stands on the axis of the Terrace Walk with steps leading to beech trees, pines, and tulip trees. The sharper red of the maples and the golden glow of tulip trees in autumn form a tapestry against the darker green background of laurel and pines. The suede-coloured leaves of oak and beech start to cover the grass. A small archway leads to a cut-stone tunnel to the walled garden dug out of the bank, and sheltered by ilex trees. Brick-backed borders of shrubs line the walls and there is a seat under the spreading magnolia. Clipped tunnels of beech are in their infancy. There are espaliered apples, and the smell of wet leaves and bonfires. Great stands of beech, and Monterey pine lead to one end of the avenue. Reeds in the Corrib in autumn grow up to the castle walls with the forest on the other side of the inlet turning amber. On rainy days the choppy grey waters of the Lough form small flecked white horses, and a splash of red gold beech leaves come down to the water's edge. Ilex, pine, and beech trees fringe the river. The whole shore seems full of little stone quays with brown water lapping against them.

Perhaps Peter Campbell appreciates most what Lord Ardilaun achieved at Ashford:

'The track of his hand is everywhere around Cong, which is a monument in itself to his profound experience and love of the place. He was always caring for and appreciating the environment, and would do nothing to harm it.'

Lady Ardilaun was appreciated, too. An old woman whom she used to visit in a tenement house in Dublin said quietly when she heard she had died:

'God rest her soul, for she was good. She would sit here without a proud end on her. She was a friend to the sick and poor.'

Edward Clifford the painter (1844–1907) was born in Bristol and was a deeply religious man much influenced by Holman Hunt. His work consisted of Biblical scenes, and portraits that he exhibited at the Royal Academy in London. In the pre-Raphaelite portrait he painted of Olive Ardilaun as a young woman she gazes thoughtfully out at the world with a calm sweet, expression (see page 81). A single dark tendril escapes from her carefully pinned hair, her eyes are violet blue, and she has tucked a red and a white carnation into the lace of her bodice. A watery landscape of islands in a Lough fringed by distant blue mountains forms the background to her portrait as it was to form the background to much of her life.

Chapter 12

Knotted Threads

Lady Ardilaun's death was the end of an era. The next occupant of Ashford Castle was a kindly and benevolent figure and the 2nd son of the 1st Earl of Iveagh, the Hon. Arthur Ernest Guinness (1876–1949).

His generation was the first of the brewery line of Guinesses to be totally educated in England, in his case at Eton and Cambridge. He married in 1903 Marie Clotilde (known as Chloe), daughter of Sir George and Lady Russell, and they had three dazzling daughters, Maureen, Aileen and Oonagh. Ernest Guinness had a boyish simplicity of character that kept him unspoilt by great possessions, and he was never heard to say an unkind word about anyone. Essentially modest and always courteous, he was rather silent in company and secretly longed to be back with the things that really interested him, such as his farm or his yacht the *Fantome* and his many mechanical and experimental instruments A friend wrote in his obituary in *The Times* of 20 April 1949:

'One thing that struck me on a yachting cruise up the coast of Alaska, was his utterly uncynical attitude to the vast number of begging letters he received. I doubt whether any deserving one was turned down'.

His wife Chloe was spirited and charming. Her mother was the author of *Mano's Memories and Memoranda*, which recounted the story of the beautiful sisters, Lady Leitrim and Lady Charlemont, who had lived at Ross Hill, an estate near Cong, and whose sons had sold it in the 1850s to the Guinesses so that the lands became part of the Ashford property.

The Hon. Ernest Guinness took no part in public life but was entirely concerned with the business of the

136

The Hon. Mrs Aileen Plunket at Luggala

Lady Dorothy Lygou holds court

Lady Oranmore and Browne, with her children, Gay and Tessa, from her first marriage at Luggala

Chapter 12

Guinness brewery in St. James' Gate, Dublin. His great-nephew is the Hon. Desmond Guinness, the son of the poet Brian Guinness, the late Lord Moyne.

Desmond was the Founder, with his late wife Mariga, of the charitable preservation group The Irish Georgian Society which raises money for the rescue and restoration of threatened Irish 18th, 19th and 20th century buildings. In the early 1960s Desmond bought and, with Mariga, saved the 18th century Castletown House in Celbridge, County Kildare. This important building had been in danger of destruction, and is now in the care of Dúchas, the Department of Arts, Culture, the Gaeltacht and the Islands. Desmond now lives at Leixlip Castle in County Kildare and remembers his great-uncle Ernest Guinness:

'He was the only one of the family in his generation who really knew the brewery well. He understood and cared about every valve and every pipe, much more so than any of his brothers. Ernest was terribly interested in engineering and electronics and had an automatic pipe organ that had a little button on the coal scuttle which, when pressed, caused the organ to slide out and start up playing *Cherry Ripe* by itself! When he ordered a boat from Campher and Nicholson he wanted it cut in half and re-adapted to his own plans. "But, Mr. Guinness," interrupted the boat builder, "that will be much more expensive than having a whole new boat." "Never mind the money," snapped the customer, "that is how I want it done".'

Ernest Guinness was a keen yachtsman, motorist and pilot, and was also the only private person in Ireland in his day to have four aeroplanes of his own, as well as fleets of boats and cars.

Piers Brendon in his book *The Head of Guinness* recounts that Ernest was an amiable host who enjoyed entertaining the junior brewers on his beautiful shooting estate at Cong where he employed over two hundred people:

'Every one of whom', he was fond of remarking, 'might fall over if you removed his (sweeping) brush.'

He loved gadgets, and practical jokes and in Dublin the family lived in Glenmaroon, the house with a walkway over the road on the way up Chapelizod Hill in Castleknock.

In London their house was on the site where the Irish Embassy is today, at number 5 Grosvenor Place. Desmond Guinness' mother, now Lady Moseley, remembers their parties—although they weren't the smartest in town, they were certainly the most fun, with the three beautiful daughters leading the dance.

However, Ernest Guinness' grand passion was the family's business. He had extensive practical experience of working in every department of the brewery where he laboured happily all his life, wearing round his waist a huge bundle of keys to all the firm's safes.

His greatest pleasure came from sailing his yacht the *Fantome*, which cruised around the Mediterranean as well as the Far East. He hated getting off the yacht and eating ashore, but one day his family persuaded him to take the great step and booked a table at a restaurant for lunch. A case of Guinness (his only drink) was sent ahead to the

Ernest Guinness' seaplane

restaurant and when they arrived a huge tureen of ice had been put on the middle of the table with all the bottles of Guinness in the middle. He took one look and roared, 'I will not drink iced Guinness', and swept back to the yacht followed by his frustrated family whom he refused to allow to have any lunch either!

All three of his beautiful daughters were heiresses and legendary hostesses. Maureen married the 4th Marquis of Dufferin and Ava, who was tragically killed in the World War II. He was the grandson of the great pro-consul, the 1st Marquis of Dufferin, who had been Viceroy of India and Governor General of Canada as well as ambassador to Russia, Turkey, Italy, and France. By the greatest fortune Maureen Guinness could afford to save Lord Dufferin's house and bankrupt estate of Clandeboye in Northern Ireland. For the remainder of her life including two more

Dismounting from the sea-plane with Ernest Guinness' daughters Oonagh and Aileen in the rowing boat that was sent to fetch them and their Pekinese dog

marriages she was always to be known as Maureen Marchioness of Dufferin and Ava.

Ernest's second daughter Aileen married Brinsley Plunket (a grandson of Lord Ardilaun's sister who had married Bishop Plunket) and was given the magical house and lands of Luttrelstown Castle in Clonsilla, County Dublin. She decorated her castle with great taste and generously hosted famous parties until all her fortune was spent.

The smallest, prettiest, and most intellectual daughter, Oonagh, who, by a curious coincidence was to marry the 4th Lord Oranmore and Browne, the great-grandson of the man who had originally sold Ashford to Sir Benjamin Lee Guinness, was given by her father Luggala, the Gothic shooting lodge of the Latouche family situated in one of the great beauty spots of County Wicklow.

Luggala stands today in the middle of a ravishingly beautiful valley ringed by vertiginous mountains and is lived in by her son, the Hon. Garech Browne, champion of Irish music both traditional and classical and the founder of the record company Claddagh and the world-famous group The Chieftains.

Oonagh would transform Luggala into a literary and artistic centre where she entertained, among others, the writer Cyril Connolly, the artist Lucian Freud, and the historian Robert Kee who dedicated his great book *The History of Ireland* to her.

Oonagh's ex-husband, the present 98-year-old Lord Oranmore and Browne, lived at Castle McGarett and remembers staying with her father at Ashford Castle when he used to shoot there in the early 1930s. He especially remembers a flight they took in Ernest Guinness' (his future father-in-law's) sea plane:

'He and I and the pilot and the cockney mechanic Trump, all took off over the Loch. "Shall we go to Glenmaroon?" Ernest asked, but then when we got up into the air it started to pour with rain, so after a tour of the Corrib we came back and landed back in front of Ashford. As we got off the plane I could hear awful curses coming from above us. Looking up I saw it was the mechanic who was climbing down from the roof simply furious. He had been forgotten on take-off and had been up there clinging to the roof all the way round the Loch. "You must be more careful next time," Ernest said severely to the pilot as we walked off.'

They all went yachting on the *Fantome* in the summer, and woodcock shooting in January:

'When we went shooting there were usually 100 beaters, many more than were required, and they continually went on strike for more money,' Lord Oranmore and Browne remembers. 'It was very luxurious staying at Ashford, and chefs were brought into the house from the yacht. Chloe, Ernest's wife, was very keen on her family tree and was a descendant of Louise de Kerouaille, mistress of King Charles II.'

Oonagh and Dom first lived at Castle Mc Garrett, 18 miles from Ashford and Desmond Guinness recalls what it was like to stay in the house there in his youth:

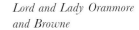

Ernest Guinness and his daughter Aileen at Ashford

'A bell rang to warn you to get ready for dinner and it was not at all like life at Knockmarroon where I had grown up which was more "nursery tea". At Castle Mc Garrett there were lovely silver birds on the table, and a silver pad and pencil for Dom to write down his thoughts and it was much the grandest house I had ever stayed in. One was in great state, and on top of that there was a lot of penny roulette which was heaven for a boy of 15.'

This was all considered very racy and fast by the more staid of the disapproving country neighbours!

So the three beautiful Guinness girls all stayed at Ashford Castle with their parents for the woodcock shooting parties and the hunt balls. Oonagh fell in love and married their near neighbour, and the other girls enjoyed whirlwind romances.

Then on one fateful day in 1939 the ghillies and beaters went on strike one time too many in the middle of the day's shooting. Just as they were preparing to carry 'the guns' over by boat to Inchigoill Island they struck for more money. Ernest Guinness had had enough. If they had done it at the beginning of the day rather than in the middle, he would have negotiated, but this was too much even for him. He abandoned the shoot and carried off 'the guns' in his aeroplanes to Scotland.

The following week Ashford Castle and the estate was up for sale. The future of the huge property hung once more in the balance.

Lord and Lady Oranmore and Browne

Chapter 13

The Quiet Man

I n 1939 22,000 acres were sold by the Iveagh
trustees to the State for £20,000—10,000 of these
acres were placed in the care of the Forestry
Service, and the remainder was divided up by the
Land Commission and sold to tenant farmers.

The hotelier Noel Huggard rented 150 acres and the
castle itself to run as a hotel. Thus, a link of almost 200
years with the Guinness family was severed by the sale, but
nevertheless the cast of characters did not entirely change,
as Lord Oranmore and Browne stepped in. He and the
Marquis of Sligo, another neighbouring landlord, rented
the contentious woodcock shooting from the Forestry
Service. For the next 50 years Lord Oranmore and Browne
with the help of many local people and especially Richard
Gibbons of Cong ran the shoot, thereby continuing his
family's almost feudal association with the area, which
stretched back even further than the Guinnesses, to the
early 18th century.

Peter Campbell tells me that from the 1920s to the
1950s, these shoots were not only sporting but also
intensely social events in the local community. Taking
place in December and January they were definite high
points in the seasonal calender by which people reckoned
what was happening in the course of the year.

To begin with, Ernest Guinness employed up to 100
beaters on each shoot, which was many more than were
needed, and they continually went on strike for more
money. After Guinness the number fell to 12 beaters and
a head beater, a gamekeeper, at least two pickers to collect,
count, and carry the fallen birds in their 'gamestick', seven
actual 'guns', a loader to stand behind each 'gun' and
no less than three dog handlers for the retrievers.

Chapter 13

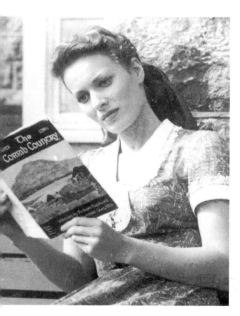

Scenes from John Ford's The Quiet Man. *Starring John Wayne and Maureen O'Hara, the film helped to put Ashford on the map*

So still a considerable body of men. The December shoot heralded the advent of Christmas, and families depended on the shoot for something for the Christmas dinner table. The shoot in January signaled the longer days at hand and was relied on for the provision of a new pair of shoes or an item of clothing badly needed. In the 1970s and 1980s young beaters looked forward to the shoots, which meant pocket money and a few days off school.

Beaters' paths were cut in the forest with two shooting paths on either side. The carefully positioned and spaced 'guns' keep pace with the beaters walking slowly in line and shooting the birds as they are flushed out by the beaters. This is what is meant by a 'driven' woodcock shoot. The powerhouse of the shoot is the gamekeeper, who is in charge of safety and organisation and is in control of birds, guns, and beaters.

The woodcock with its long beak, bright eyes, and pointed pin feathers is a prize worthy of only the best shots, since in flight it wheels and zig-zags through the trees making it the most difficult of all game birds to hit. Little is really known about the species, but Peter Campbell says that no wet woodcock has ever been shot. Woodcocks have an inbuilt uncanny judgement of the weather and they appear to be at least two days' ahead of any adverse change.

By the end of the 19th century all the tree planting done by Lord Ardilaun was beginning to pay dividends. His coverts, together with the natural hazel, started to attract the prized woodcock in large numbers. The continuous influx of game birds prompted the idea of a really well organised, well-run 'driven woodcock shoot', which was pretty unique in Europe at the time.

All these plans culminated in the great day on 25 January 1905 when the Prince of Wales attended the opening shoot, which lasted for five days with six other 'guns' and a successful bag of 462 woodcock. Everything went like clockwork to Lord Ardilaun's intense relief. The fine stands of commercial timber and the beautiful arboreta were, according to Peter Campbell, 'shining examples that good forestry and good shooting were not incompatible'.

A record for one day's shoot in Great Britain and Ireland for seven guns with a bag of 236 birds was established at Cong on 31 January 1910, and is noted in the Guinness Book of Records. The 'guns' were their host, Lord Bandon, Mr E. Becker, Mr C. P. Coote, The O'Connor Don, Percy La Touche. and the Hon. E. O'Brien. When Lord Oranmore and Browne took over the shoot in 1940 he established a syndicate whose guest lists were peppered with the names of some of the best as well as the most aristocratic shots in the world, all of whom competed eagerly for a mid-winter invitation to the wilder shores of the Corrib.

As well as his Irish neighbours, the Duke of Devonshire, Signor Chiano (who shot for Italy in Mexico in 1968), the Duke of Grafton, Prince d'Arenberg, Prince de Caraman Chimay, Monsieur L'Abbe de la Motte, Count de Ganay, Count de Gramont, Monsieur Alain de Rothschild,

Mr. Raymond Guest, the O'Connor Don, the Marquis of Dufferin and many others made their way to the woodlands where, as Lord Ardilaun had wisely planned, the best woodcock shooting in the world was to be enjoyed.

'The best shot of all,' remembers Lord Oranmore and Browne, 'was Purdey Coote, and Jean Louis de Ganay came a very good second.' Over the years the woodcock have become rarer, and in the 1980s the Oranmore and Browne connection came to an end. Now, the shoot itself has been amalgamated with the pheasant shooting at Dromoland Castle in County Clare, the sister hotel of Ashford Castle.

By the beginning of World War II Noel Huggard, a keen fisherman and hotelier from the Butler Arms, Waterville, County Kerry, had leased Ashford Castle and was busy running it primarily as a fishing hotel. It was a far smaller enterprise than today and some guests would stay for three weeks.

Noel Huggard was a good business man and watched for every opportunity to make the venture a success. Denis Lenihan, the current executive chef of the hotel, tells how one of Noel's ideas that worked particularly well was his planning of the fish menu.

Noel would get up at around 5am and nip down to the kitchen to check the guests' catch in the refrigerator from the day before. Then he would quickly plan his meals, gut the fish, and have them laid out prepared and ready for the menus. By the time the guests woke up and were about to leave, it would be too late for them to decide to take their fish with them—if they wanted to eat them they would have to stay for dinner!

Mrs. Sheila Wilson Wright, a Blosse Lynch from Partry House, remembers growing up as a neighbour to Ashford, when her mother ran a market garden during the War and supplied the hotel in summer with fruit and vegetables. She remembers her days as a child in the West:

'There was an open door at home to everyone and not just for two nights but people always stayed for a week or two. There was petrol rationing, so getting to the West was a real endeavour. You had to get off the train at Claremorris and change into a little train to do the two stops to Ballinrobe. We went to church on Sundays in a pony and trap; tied up the pony in the pub; tacked up, and then went home afterwards.'

The Lynch side of Sheila's family were one of the Tribes of Galway and she recalls the story of the window where a mayor of Galway hanged his son, who was due to be tried in court for killing a man in a dual—hence the verb 'to lynch'.

'They lived very simple lives in keeps and were quite rough and tough,' she says of her ancestors. 'Life was very feudal, transport didn't exist, and there was a lot of intermarriage with people marrying and intermarrying within a distance of 30 or 40 miles.'

One Lynch had ten sons and six daughters and all the sons shared the front bedroom in the dower house. Of the ten sons, three went abroad and started a shipping company on the Tigris and Euphrates, shipping the Mail

Lord Dorchester and a
friend enjoy a day's shooting

The breathtaking stained glass windows of Christ Triumphant, The Annunciation, and other Biblical scenes were executed in 1933 for the Catholic Church in Cong by the great Irish stained glass artist, Harry Clarke

from the Mediterranean to India across the desert before the cutting of the Suez Canal. Another Lynch started the famous vineyard of Lynch-Bages in France. As neighbours, Ashford Castle—whether as a private house or a hotel— always played an important part in their family lives.

It was during Noel Huggard's day in the early 1950s that one of the great coincidences took place that was to secure Ashford Castle hotel a permanent place in the affections of many millions of people all over the world.

The late and great Lord Killanin lived nearby at Oughterard and, while in the British Army during the last years of the Japanese war in 1937/8 had become friends with the American film director John Ford. He also knew the work of writer Maurice Walsh from Listowel, County Kerry.

Back home, he and John Ford kept in touch and a few years later John Ford sent him a script of a Maurice Walsh story written by Frank Nugent, the film critic on *The New York Times*. Ford wanted to make it into a film. The story was of wealthy returning Irish exile Sean Thornton to the cottage, White O'Morn, where he had been born, and his love for Mary Kate Danaher, his proposal and the refusal of the proposal by her brother Red Will Danaher with whom he has been competing to buy his old family home from the widow Dillane.

The twists and turns of the story are heightened by the most dramatic shots of Ashford scenery, culminating in the rousing fight with Will Danaher, and the final reconciliation and happy ending. There were great opportunities for wonderful character sketches of the Parish Priest Father Lonigan who loves fishing, and the Church of Ireland rector, the Rev. Mr. Playfair, an ex-boxer from Cambridge University.

Lord Killanin read the script with mounting enthusiasm. The director wanted to make the film based on Spiddal, but Killanin thought the best place would be Noel Huggard's hotel and the lovely locations around it. The siting of the hotel in some of the most beautiful scenery in the west of Ireland sealed the decision.

Lord Killanin chose all the locations, spotting the red bridge near Kylemore Abbey, and the bridge near Maam on his way back to Oughterard, and chosing the beloved tower of the poet W. B. Yeats at Thor Ballylee as a background against which John Wayne and the impossibly beautiful Maureen O'Hara would charge across the river and shelter from a thunderstorm in a cut-stone ruined doorway. His shirt and her dress glisten in the downpour as they get satisfactorily soaked to the skin and the music reaches a crescendo of enthusiasm as they stand clasped in each others arms.

The facades of houses and pubs in Cong, Clonbur, and other locations in the area were all chosen for their picturesque qualities and for their proximity to the hotel. Killanin said that he always thought of *The Quiet Man* as a 'Western' that happened to be made in Ireland. Although each personality is larger than life, there is nevertheless such brilliant acting and characterisation in each vignette, and more than a grain of such well-observed truth in each character, that we all want to be swept away back into those safe comfortable days that almost but perhaps never quite existed.

The eternal story of the returning Irish exile is played by John Wayne as Sean Thornton, although whether everyone succeeds in meeting a shapely Maureen O'Hara herding her unlikely flock of sheep among the trees of Lord Ardilaun's park is open to question!

Nevertheless the film is an enthralling period piece with the widow Dillane with 'neither chick nor child but good to the poor' having real 18th century Irish furniture in her simulated parlour and ending up in an unlikely pairing with Red Will, Squire Danaher, Mary Kate's brother and the ferocious foe of Sean Thornton in what must be one of the longest and most enjoyable fights in cinema history.

The whole village of Cong was turned into a film set with hundreds of local extras and every single villager pressed into service. After the general melee and rush of the huge crowd down the hill during the fight scenes there were several sore ribs the next day. There was an awful to-do with the real-life Church of Ireland rector when the stone font from the Catholic Church in Cong was borrowed and used as a stoop for holy water. This played an important role in 'the patti-fingers' incident between Sean Thornton and Mary Kate Danaher outside Lord Ardilaun's Protestant Church which was 'pretending' to be the Catholic Church in the film, but it was left behind, to the highly insulted fury of the rector. Brilliant actors from the Abbey Theatre in Dublin such as Eileen Crow, Jack MacGowran of Beckett fame, and Arthur Shields, were every bit as good as the big stars.

John Wayne borrowed Lord Killanin's black hunter to ride, but when the star said, 'What a bloody awful horse' they realised he had never ridden without a western saddle before, so one had to be sent for from America. Etta Vaughan O'Sullivan was Maureen O'Hara's stand-in and remembers that 200 girls from all over Ireland applied for the job. It took hours and hours to do a five-minute shot. John Ford was a perfectionist and, as well as that, there was no electricity, so a generator had to be positioned half a mile away to deaden the noise. Maureen O'Hara is a fiery red-head in real life as well as in the film and occasionally wore the most lovely and nostalgic Aran-knitted berets over her glossy locks.

The film company paid £600 to use the shop front of Cunane's pub, which in reality was a sweet shop and grocery store while all interiors were set up in the studio back in Hollywood. John Wayne smoked cigarettes furiously against the background of Ashford, while the adorable Barry FitzGerald as Micheleen Oge smoked his pipe in his pony and trap. Except during suitably dramatic moments the sun always shone.

Each day's filming would be packed up and sent back to America in the evening and back would come 600-word telegrams to the astonishment of the postmistress. Forty years on, the folklore in Cong about the making of the film is every bit as potent as any medieval tale. John Ford's sentimental journey back in time to the basics of Irish rural life had turned into a film that was to become a classic. Fortunately for Ashford Castle, *The Quiet Man* industry had begun!

From that day on, news of the hotel and its location spread, and when Noel Huggard retired and John A.

Mulcahy took over he felt confident enough about its future to expand into more rooms, and to build the golf course where once the Ardilauns' drive had meandered through gentle sloping parkland down to the shores of the the Corrib.

One of the other great attractions of Ashford has always been the fishing. Frank Costello is the head fishing ghillie, as his father was before him from 1937–1974. His father taught him to fish when Frank was about seven and he hasn't stopped since!

He tells me that the Corrib was always famous for wild brown trout and salmon, and that they can easily equal the 24lb record for a fish. The season opens on the 15 February for trout and salmon, and goes right through to 30 September. The Corrib has always been famous for its Mayfly season and May is the best month for dapping (catching the natural Mayfly which are hooked onto the line). June would be the best month for catching the most salmon, and June and July are excellent for dry-fly fishing on the water in the evenings.

In August dragonflies and grasshoppers are again used for dapping and in September the wet-fly fishing improves again. Because of weather changes due to global warming the June and July fishing, which would have been slow for wet-fly, is gradually changing. A fisherman might catch ten or 15 trout in the Mayfly season and if you caught four or five salmon in a day you would be very pleased indeed.

The fish are bigger because there is more feeding for them now, but it is less predictable because of the changeable weather. The most important thing nowadays is that the ghillies encourage a catch-and-release system although if you do want to keep your fish, as always, the chefs in the hotel will cook it for your dinner! During a day on the water it is traditional to stop on an island and boil a kettle to make a cup of tea and eat a picnic.

The Cong river is very good for salmon and is kept as a private beat for the hotel guests. There is very good salmon fishing there in April, May, and June with fly and spinning—Frank Costello has heard of two people fishing in a boat who brought home a catch of 36 trout! That was with two men fishing and two men rowing.

The hotel has boats for hire and can arrange for hotel guests to fish in other lakes around Connemara as well. Be warned that fishing stories in all the pubs in Cong abound!

Right, J. F. Fuller's fortifications in the garden
Left, John Wayne and Maureen O'Hara enjoy the scenery
around Cong during the filming of The Quiet Man

Chapter 14

Tapestry Completed

While Walter Curley was the American Ambassador to Ireland in the 1970s he had many opportunities to come to the West and visited Ashford with American, French, and Irish friends, becoming more and more impressed with its special atmosphere of antiquity, solitude and beauty. When, in 1985, the owner of Ashford, John A. Mulcahy decided to sell his hotel, Ambassador Curley had by then retired to private life. He and a few friends and relatives and several fellow venture capitalists formed a syndicate of about two dozen people to purchase the property. The syndicate made renovations to the castle, redecorated some of the interiors, and created a driven pheasant and duck shoot that enabled the hotel to extend the spring and summer season into autumn and winter. And so, yet again, a new chapter in the Ashford Castle story was to begin.

Over the next 16 years the hotel continued on its successful way under the current ownership of well-known Irish American business executives and business owners. There are seven members of the Board of Directors under the current Chairmanship of Kevin Crowe. 'I feel very fortunate,' the Chairman tells me, 'that we are able to be the custodians of this wonderful and historic castle and estate, and we intend to preserve its past glory and future position as one of the premier properties in the world.'

The owners have invested millions of pounds in the upkeep of the fabric of the buildings and in the development of the grounds in the hope that in another 800 years time Ashford Castle will be as much appreciated as it is today! This seems highly likely as for the last eight years in a row the hotel has been voted the number one in Ireland

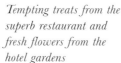

Tempting treats from the superb restaurant and fresh flowers from the hotel gardens

and according to *Gourmet Magazine* in its May 1999 issue Ashford Castle is listed as the number one hotel in the world in The Design\Architecture Award section and was named the best hotel overall for the whole of Britain and Ireland. It was also listed in the Condé Nast *Traveller* of January 1999 in its Gold List as one of the best places to stay in the world!

The luxury and comfort inside the castle contrasts sharply with the daunting outside facade of cut-stone cliff-like walls with their battlements and arrow-loops. The ground-floor saloons are hung with huge blue Japanese Imari dishes against pale blue watered-silk walls. Coloured glass lanterns create pools of light, and Waterford crystal chandeliers glimmer in the Connaught Room. A gleaming Irish bright-cut grate surrounds the hall fireplace. *Food & Wine Magazine* declares the reception rooms as 'almost large enough to land a small private jet'. The panelled hall has a gallery that runs all around the first floor, edged with Victorian turned banisters where the band once played for Lady Ardilaun's dances. There is a misty picture of the West of Ireland with the ruins of Donegal Abbey painted by Patrick Vincent Duffy 1832–1909 and a painting of a pretty Victorian lady in a red velvet dress and hat and diaphanous shawl looking out from her frame on the ever changing picture of the fountain against the lake and the battlements that edge the Lough. In one of the halls an arm-chair stands next to an Edwardian chessboard inlaid into a table and makes a comfortable position from which to view the world going by. Receptionists in their red jackets are showing the arriving guests to their rooms; dinner hostesses in dark jackets leading the party for tea to their seats; baggage handlers darting here and there; while the chambermaids in blue-and-white striped uniforms are bustling through the corridors giving an effect that is both purposeful and enormously pleasant. There are still superbly high standards of service and the staff are patient, friendly and pleasant. There are welcoming faces at every turn, and no one is allowed to go unrecognised or unacknowledged. Assistant Manager Michael Duggan sees that everything humanly possible is done to make guests feel at home and there are so many reception rooms that large groups meld in, while individuals do not feel swamped. Soon the dinner will begin in the two dining-rooms as guests unwind after their days in the open air.

Ashford Castle Hotel today is world-renowned for its *haute cuisine*. Denis Lenihan, chef for 24 years at the Castle, tells me that on any one evening they might have guests in the dining-room who had come from as many as 14 different countries so the food has to have an international accent. 'The world has become such a small place and we have seen huge changes in the food since I first began'. Today he tells me that the food is about quality and consistency, so that when guests come back again and again they need to know what to expect. 'Quite a few staff members have been here for a number of years and it makes for a great structure. A chef's job today is a mixture of being an artist, a chef, and a manager,' he explains. He tries to source as much food as he can in the locality using organic vegetables, and local meat and fish. 'The production of food in the West is still very "green" and unintensified but all the same you are not going to find kangaroo in the west of Ireland,' he jokes.

When he first came to the hotel there were eight chefs in the kitchen and the hotel was only open for six months of the year. Now it is open all year round and 20 chefs are at work full time. They still buy from the same butcher and greengrocer, which makes for a very good, consistent product. 'There was a Lenihan here as chef to the Guinnesses 100 years ago,' he tells me, and his own grandfather was chef here as well. The wheel of Ashford Castle life in all departments continues to turn and the food in the hotel is of a consistently high quality, which the rows and rows of the many recent awards of excellence that hang in the hall, the dining-room, and in the memorabilia room confirm. Denis is a widower and lives behind the golf course with his two children, Stephen aged 13, and Ruth aged 10. Perhaps this hotel may be lucky enough to have become a family hotel in more ways than one! Outside in the bay the little islands change their configurations as you walk through the *enfilade* of ground floor reception rooms past the windows of this amazingly long building looking out at the ever-changing view of tree-tufted islands against the waters of the lake. In the Inglenook dining-room with a fire burning brightly in the grate you are cosily enclosed by the wooden shelves of what was once Lord Ardilaun's library. The carved wooden heads of Dante and Helen of Troy smile their secret smiles on the corbels either side of the fireplace.

The Connaught Room is the castle's award-winning gourmet restaurant. At night the Waterford crystal chandeliers glow against the darkening window panes as the damask table cloths and linen napkins on the tables tempt the diners to sit down and give their orders. The larger wood-panelled George V dining-room overlooks the gate house and the river, which rushes out under the bridge and into the Lough. Great windows flood the room with light letting in the landscape.

The laying of the tables is exquisite with a vase of fresh flowers for each table, and Peter Cullen and Seamus Judge, the expert Maitre d's, keep a cool and polished command over this empire. The food is delicious and each course an irresistible treat. Leaving the table with a plate unfinished feels a sin.

'I just might have one more glass of wine,' I remark.

'A bird never flew on one wing,' Peter Cullen replies comfortingly, as he whisks away my empty bottle. I think to myself that perhaps good dialogue comes naturally to the race that bred *The Quiet Man*. The wine list actually makes far more interesting reading than many a modern novel and offers some marvellous opportunities to drink extremely well. The great houses are all here, but not at the expense of wines from the lower end of the scale, and some splendid and reasonably priced champagne. The Sommelier clearly understands his subject thoroughly.

For horse lovers there is no better place to experience the thrill of riding Irish, with the adrenaline rush of

Chandelier made in Waterford and Boulle Clock reflected in a Roccoco gilt mirror

Chapter 14

A monster fish makes a good story at any time

adventure by day followed by the salve of ancient luxury and feasting by night, than at Ashford Castle. The wild roots of the Irish fox-hunting tradition are still a celebration of battlefield virtue stemming from the days of a warrior class that revelled in mud-smeared risk and violence. Cross-country riding and fox-hunting are among the many sports that guests can enjoy while staying at the hotel, and the equestrian centre is run by Tim and Bridget Clesham in the grounds. Tim and Bridget Clesham's families have lived in County Mayo for generations, and they keep and breed Connemara ponies said to descend from the herd that swam ashore from the wrecked ships of the Spanish Armada. The Connemara pony is the best type of horse in their opinion. 'He's quicker to learn than the bigger horse and more sure-footed while noticing

everything that is going on around him. He may shy and look at things, but he keeps going forward and he has the ability to quickly get you out of trouble, a quality known in Ireland as a horses' fifth leg,' reports Tim. 'The Irish people are associated with horses more than any other people in the world,' he explains and his Irish hunters can take you galloping over the 3,000 acres of what was the ancient Ashford deer park between Loughs Corrib and Mask without ever having to go outside the grounds. Crossing the main roads is cleverly dealt with by riding under them in the tunnels specially provided by the foresight of Lord Ardilaun! Beginners are catered for by a gentle introduction to the sport, and it is at the equestrian centre that world-renowned Olympic rider Captain Mark Phillips, ex-husband of the Princess Royal

152

of England, runs his hunting clinic several times a year. A cross-country day on horseback guided by the equestrian centre's able staff affords magical glimpses of woods and hedgerows, hills and streams, and sometimes of the stone foundations of groups of 19th century houses in 'Famine Villages' next to their poignant ridges of abandoned potato plots. There were always horses for riding at Ashford and the equestrian centre today is an example of yet another ancient tradition that continues in the demesne.

In 1999 James and Deborah Knight opened Ireland's first School of Falconry in the old cobbled farmyard, which used to be the hub of the farm. The beautiful stone buildings were restored and converted into luxurious accommodation for hawks, falcons, buzzards, owls, and an eagle. Falconers for ten years, the Knights run a variety of lessons, hawk walks, and hunting sessions during which guests step back in time to learn how to 'cast' their hawk off into trees and recall it to land on their gloved fist.

As well as learning the history of falconry, they also learn a little of how the birds are trained and used for hunting. James Knight tells me, 'No-one ever forgets the moment when a hawk first lands on their gloved fist because opportunities to experience, up close, one of nature's most awe-inspiring predators are rare.'

Falconers become very attached to their birds despite the fact that these feelings are not reciprocated. A hawk will become familiar with the falconer and there is a bond and trust that exists between them, but the hawk will have no loyalty or affection for the falconer and never becomes a pet. Equally, the hawk has no aggression toward the falconer, viewing him as a business partner and a valuable aid to finding food. This unique relationship takes time and skill to achieve and falconers, by necessity, become quite obsessive about their art. Irish falcons have a great reputation. In the 11th century Gerald of Wales wrote his famous book *The History and Topography of Ireland*, in which he states, 'this country above any other produces hawks, falcons and sparrowhawks abundantly. These birds have been provided by nature with courageous heart, curved and sharp beaks, and feet armed with talons, most suitable for catching their prey.'

The most practical species flown would have been the native Peregrine falcon catching waterfowl and grouse and the Goshawk catching rabbits, hares, and game birds. Today the Goshawk has vanished from the Irish countryside, but Peregrine falcons nest only 15 minutes away on land once belonging to Ashford. It is inconceivable that the monks of Cong Abbey and the Norman de Burgos did not have Peregrine falcons. Apart from snares this would have been their only method of catching game. The spirits of the monks and Norman knights of long ago must surely be comforted to hear once again the jingle of hawk bells around the grounds!

Brown trout from the Corrib on the lake shore

Golf is another sport that guests practise from morning till night on the shamrock-green links that flow down to the shoreline, and in the hotel shop there is all the panoply of golfing regalia engraved and printed with the Ashford Castle logo. Also stocked in the shop are brightly coloured throws, handsome jackets and caps made in the specially woven Ashford Castle tweed, coats and jerseys, crisp linen, and the Ashford Castle silk scarf designed by Carlton Varney. Table mats, watercolours of the castle, and cuff links bearing the initial "A" in entwined letters topped with a plump coronet are all on sale as well.

One of the greatest joys of Ashford are the magnificent grounds, acres of which had been more or less allowed to run wild over the many years since the Guinness family left. In 1996 the Board of Directors of Ashford Castle took a key decision to shoulder the responsibility to make every effort to restore Lady Ardilaun's gardens and walks to their former glory. They invested thousands of pounds in clearing away undergrowth and planting trees, and Arthur Shackleton was employed to make a report using the old Ordinance Survey maps of 1845 and 1899 and plans of the original tracery of the plantings, the buildings, and the paths. Fortunately he found photographs *circa* 1900 in the National Archives as well, and the Board enthusiastically decided to go ahead with the proposed restoration.

This was to be a huge decision and already a very noticeable change has taken place in a very short space of time. The magnificent Broad Walk, which runs parallel to the Lough and is a very wide and very long impressive

Captain Mark Phillips runs regular hunting and cross-country clinics at Ashford

Chapter 14

walk bordered by pines, had been encroached upon so that between fallen trees and riotous undergrowth, the sides had shrunk in. This has all now been cleared with the wide lawns reinstated on the sides of the path and missing trees replanted that had originally been there. The Terrace Walk, which was probably once the original formal front avenue, has also had lots of missing trees replaced; inappropriate planting removed, and flights of steps renewed, so that the full uninterrupted majesty of its structure can now be clearly seen. The walled garden where Andrew Campbell had raised all his specimen plants was completely derelict, abandoned, and run down. All the potting sheds and buildings have since been re-roofed and brought back to their present good condition with the brick paths, stone walls, and borders reinstated, and a hornbeam tunnel, box hedges, espaliered fruit trees, and herbaceous borders planted. The drawbridge leading to the Woodland Walk was repaired and the walk re-opened from being found on the original maps after being closed for many years.

Hundreds of large trees such as Chestnuts, Beech, Oaks, and Limes as well as Tulip trees, and Walnuts have been replanted, and all the gardens and garden buildings are in wonderful trim. Many of the wall and turret structures in the gardens immediately beside the house appear on first sight as fragments of Victorian castle-style architecture, that have somehow become detached from the main building but James Howley the architect and author of *The Follies and Garden Buildings of Ireland* considers them to be part of the garden. 'On re-appraising these structures,' he writes 'I now acknowledge them to be a good deal more subtle than I had first guessed, and they provide valuable and interesting garden scenery to set off, or frame the main castle building in a most impressive and eye-catching manner.' They have been sensitively restored as has the very fragile arch-way with the two Ionic hermes supporting the entablature and cornice that frames the entrance to the curving rockwork tunnel leading into the walled garden. The round turret or redout on the water has been cleared, mended, and re-pointed with proper lime mortar, and provides a delightful vantage point from which one can look back to enjoy views of the castle, or else in the other direction out over the Lough and countryside beyond. Great gardens are not only important for their horticulture but also for the architecture of their lay-out and for the ornamental buildings which adorn them. The splendours of the pattern and landform around the grounds can now clearly be seen framed once more by the traditional planting. These grounds are now enjoyed by the many visitors who flock to the castle from all over the world. The peace and solitude of the great walks have played their part before now in the deliberations of politicians, and in the late summer of August 1998 Ashford Castle

A tawny eagle prepares to take off over the Corrib

Peter Cullen, one of the expert Maitre d's keeps a cool and polished command over the gourmet restaurant

was chosen by An Taoiseach Bertie Ahern and British Prime Minister Tony Blair as the venue to meet and re-affirm their commitment to lasting peace in Northern Ireland. The contrast with the devastated landscape of Omagh after the bomb explosion; which the British Prime Minister had visited the day before could not have been more stark. The weather at Ashford was perfect and after the meeting Prime Minister Blair looked out at the peaceful view over Lough Corrib and said admiringly, 'Now I can see why they say Mayo is magic.' A few minutes later his helicopter arrived to sweep him away to Horan International Airport to catch the plane back to London. Ashford Castle had played a special part in providing a totally secure ambience away from the turbulent current of international politics where two world leaders could meet to plan for a more hopeful future for both of their countries.

Perhaps there were echoes in this visit of the day fourteen years earlier that the President of the United States and Mrs. Reagan stayed at Ashford for two nights in June 1984 to collect his honorary degree from the University of Galway and be made a Freeman of the City. On flying through a rainbow to arrive at Shannon airport his speech to President Hillery and the assembled dignitaries blended friendship, kinship, and a yearning for peace. The singing of the National Anthem accompanied by the pipe band and military band of the Southern Command.and a 21-gun salute was to follow. President Reagan's speech made it clear that he wanted to be in Ireland to show that the land of his ancestors was dear to him. Soon he was aloft in his helicopter on his way to Cong to fly over the West and the green fields of Ireland that he made clear were close to his heart.

Back at Ashford the security was tight with a thousand-strong security force including members of the elite Marine Corps whose special task it is to guard the President. They had practically sealed off the village of Cong from the outside world since 6am that morning. The newspapers reported that Mrs. Reagan was 63 years young and 'looked youthful and trim as a fashion model'. Her first concern was always for her husband who 'always had a word for everyone. He is powerfully built, walks with certainty, and is always on the watch to make a comment

President Reagan and Mrs. Reagan stayed at Ashford Castle during their visit to Ireland in 1984

Rory Murphy, Manager of the Ashford Castle Hotel

or spot something remarkable,' reported the *Irish Independent* on Saturday, 2 June 1984. The visit was an outstanding success and the evening of their arrival they entertained the Minister for Foreign Affairs and Mrs Barry to smoked salmon and a light salad in their private suite '221' allotted to them on the ground floor for security reasons. They were following a light schedule in order to be able to absorb the atmosphere of the President's ancestral country and a turf fire had been especially lit, which was the first he had ever seen. Some of the headlines in the newspapers read 'Asleep In A Castle as 1,000 Stand Guard', 'King Cong And Queen Of The Castle', 'Dr. Reagan, Galway's New Citizen', 'Ashford Castle Becomes the White House', and many more. On the Sunday his helicopter flew the Presidential couple to the village of Ballyporeen in Tipperary, the home of his ancestors, and many still remember the moving programme on the television that day recording his arrival. He was later whisked to Dublin and a State Banquet with An Taoiseach in St. Patrick's Hall and the next morning he became only the second person to address a joint session of the Houses of the Oireachtas (Irish Parliament)—President Kennedy was the first. Not all visitors to Ashford Castle have to face the barrage of international publicity that follows Presidents and Prime Ministers but many famous people including film stars and royalty have stayed quietly at Ashford over the years. Starting with John Wayne and Maureen O'Hara during the making of *The Quiet Man*; later Princess Grace and Prince Ranier; more recently Prince Edward; Bob Hope was a frequent visitor; and the continuing list is endless of stars of stage and screen, famous business tycoons, politicians of all nationalities and persuasions, and many international sporting celebrities. Dr. Tony O'Reilly tells me, 'Ashford means Ireland. When you top the hill and look down at the castle and the glorious lake you know you are home'.

The ancient Irish tradition of princely hospitality at Ashford Castle continues today as it has done over the centuries. The castle and grounds are intact, beautifully maintained and cared for, with their future assured. The tapestry is completed.

Dante keeps watch over the comings and goings at the hotel

In 1998 An Taoiseach Bertie Ahern and Prime Minister Tony Blair chose Ashford Castle as the venue to re-affirm their commitment to peace in Northern Ireland

Bibliography

Anon (B), Herbaceous Lobelias, *Irish Gardening* Vol. III, Jan–Dec. 1912, p.139

Anon, *The Saxon in Ireland*, London, 1852

Ardilaun Lady, Obituary of Andrew Campbell. *Irish Gardening*, Vol. XIII, Jan-Dec.1918, p.13

Ball, C. F., Current Topics, *Irish Gardening*, Vol. V, Nov. 1916, p.163

Beaufort, Daniel Augustus, Extract from his itinerary in Galway and Mayo for October 6th, 1787, Beaufort MSS, Trinity College, Dublin K657(A027)

Belton, W., *The Angler in Ireland*, Vol. 1, London, 1834

Bence-Jones, Mark, *Twilight of the Ascendancy*, London, 1987

Bourke, Eamonn, *People and Places*, Whitegate, 1990

Brendon, Piers, *Head of Guinness*, Trowbridge, 1979

Byrne, Al, *Guinness Times*, Dublin, 1999

Campbell, Andrew, The Flower Garden , *Irish Gardening*, Vol. II, Jan - Dec. 1907, p.193

Campbell, Andrew, Annuals and their Culture, *Irish Gardening*, Vol. I, Mar-Dec. 1906

Campbell, Peter, Driven Woodcock Shoots at Cong, *Irish Forestry*, Vol. 41, No.1, 1984, pp.30-35

Castletown Lord, *Ego*, London, 1923

Collins, M. E., *Conquest and Colonisation*, Dublin, 1969

Coulter, Henry, *The West of Ireland, its conditions, its people*, Dublin, 1862

Crook, J. Mordaunt, *The Rise of the Nouveaux Riches*, London, 1999

Dolley, Michael, *Anglo-Norman Ireland*, Dublin, 1972

Donnelan, Sheila, William Wilde: A Father of Some Importance , Connemara, *Journal of the Clifden and Connemara Heritage Group*, Vol. 2, No.1, 1995, pp.61-67

Everett, Katherine, *Bricks and Flowers*, London, 1949

Everett, Nigel, *An Irish Arcadia: the Historic Gardens of Bantry House*, Bantry, 1999

Everett, Nigel, *Wild Gardens The Lost Demesnes of Bantry Bay*, County Cork 2000

Fahy, J. A., *The Glory of Cong*, Galway, 1986

Foster, R.F., *W. B. Yeats A Life*, Vol. 1, Oxford, 1997

Foster, R. F., *The Oxford History of Ireland*, Oxford, 1989

Frazier, Adrian, *George Moore 1852-1933*, London, 2000

Froude, J. A., *Short Studies of Great Subjects*, Vol. 3, London, 1888

Garner, William, *Galway Architectural Heritage*, National Heritage Inventory, Dublin, 1985

Gillespie, Raymond, and Moran, Gerard (editors), *A Various Country, Essays in Mayo History 1500-1900*, Westport, 1987

Graves, Charles, *Ireland Revisited*, London, no date

Greene, Mariana, *Riding Irish, Polo Magazine*, May/June 1998

Guinness, Michelle, *The Guinness Spirit*, London, 1999

Harding, Mike, *Footloose in the West of Ireland*, London, 1996

Hart-Davis, Rupert, *The Letters of Oscar Wilde*, London, 1962

Hayward, Richard, *The Corrib Country*, Dundalk, 1993

Hayward, Richard, *This is Ireland Connacht and the City of Galway*, London, 1952

Hone, Joseph, *The Life of George Moore*, London, 1936

Howley, James, *Outline Proposals For The Garden Buildings Ashford Castle Demesne, Cong, Co.Mayo*, September 1996

Kinealy, Christine, *This Great Calamity, the Irish Famine 1845-52*, Dublin, 1994

Lavelle, The Rev. Patrick, *The Irish Landlord Since the Revolution*, Dublin, 1970

Lynch, Patrick, and Vaizey, John, *Guinness' Brewery in the Irish Economy 1759-1876*, Cambridge, 1960

MacCarthy, Michael J. F., *Five Years in Ireland 1895-1900*, Hodges Figgis & Co., Dublin, 1901

Macdonell-Garvey, Maire, *Mid-Connacht*, Manor Hamilton, 1995

McDowell, R.B., *Crisis and Decline The Fate of the Southern Unionists*, Dublin, 1997

MacGearailt, Gearoid, *Celts and Normans*, Dublin, 1969

MacLochlainn, Alf, *Documents on Social Life: Four Letters from the Wilson-Lynch Papers*

Mahon, Katie, Astonishing Ashford, *Food & Wine Magazine*, September 1999.

Journal of the Galway Archeological and Historical Society, Vol. 42, 1989-90, pp133-136

MacMahon, Brian, *Here's Ireland*, London, 1971

Malcomson, Anthony, *Introduction and Calendar of the Clements of Killadoon Papers for Ross Hill*, PRONI, Belfast, draft copy, 1998

Malins, Edward, and Bowe, Patrick, *Irish Gardens and Demesnes from 1830*, London, 1980

Martelli, George, *A Man Of His Time A Life of the First Earl of Iveagh*, London, 1956

Melvin, Patrick, The Composition of the Galway Gentry, *The Irish Genealogist*, Vol. 7, No.1, 1986, pp81-96

Melvin, Patrick, *The Galway Tribes as Landowners and Gentry*, Galway History and Society, Dublin, 1996

Melvin, Patrick, *The Social Life of the Galway Gentry*, PHD Thesis, Trinity College, Dublin

Moody, T. W., and Martin, F. X. (editors), *The Course of Irish History*, Cork, 1984

Moore, George, *A Communication to My Friends*, London, 1933

Moore, George, *Parnell and His Island*, London, 1887

Moran, Gerard, Landlord and Tenant Relations in Ireland Sir Arthur Guinness and his estate at Ashford Castle 1868–1882, *Cathair naMart*, Vol. 10, No.1. 1990, pp69-88

Moran, Gerard (editor), *Galway History and Society*, Dublin, 1996

Murphy, Daniel J. (editor), *Lady Gregory's Journals 1916-1925*, Vol. I, Gerrards Cross, 1978

Murphy, J. J., *Guide to The Quiet Man*, no date

Nally, Fergal, *History of Ashford Castle*, no date

Nelson, E. Charles, *An Irish Flower Garden Replanted*, Dublin, 1997

Nelson, E. Charles, It Died On Me—The Perilous Lives of Ireland's Garden Plant , *Moorea*, Vol. 10, p.37

Nelson, E. Charles, and Brady, Aidan (editors), *Irish Gardening and Horticulture*, Dublin, 1979.

O'Brien, Mary and Connor Cruise, *A Concise History of Ireland*, London, 1972

O'Corrain, Donncha, *Ireland Before The Normans*, Dublin, 1972

O'Dowd, Peadar, *Old and New Galway*, Galway, 1985

S Fiach, Thomas, The Patriot Priest of Partry Patrick Lavelle 1825–1886, *Journal of the Galway Archeological and Historical Society*, Vol. 35, 1976, pp145-148

O'Hara (of Lenaboy), Lieutenant Colonel James, *A Lay of Ashford*, Dublin, c.1869

O'Hara (of Lenaboy), Lieutenant Colonel James, *The Cruise of the Caroline to Greece and the Greek Islands*, Dublin, 1861

O Hara (of Lenaboy), Lieutenant Colonel James, *The Cruise of the Mary Smith to Iceland*, Dublin, c.1862.

O'Leary, Con, *A Wayfarer in Ireland*, London, 1935

O'Lochlainn, Colm, *Wilde's Loch Corrib*, Dublin, no date

O'Sullivan, M. D., *Old Galway*, Cambridge, 1942.

Patterson and Kempster, *Schedule of Bills of Quantities and Measurement for Ashford Castle and Demense1872–1885*, Irish Architectural Archive.

Praeger, Robert Lloyd, *The Way That I Went*, Dublin, 1937

Quinn, J. F., *History of Mayo*, Vol. 3, Ballina, 1996

Richardson, Douglas Scott, *Gothic Revival Architecture in Ireland*, Vol. 2, New York, 1983

Robinson, Lennox (editor), *Lady Gregory's Journals* 1916-1930, New York, 1947

Robinson, Tim (editor), *Thomas Colville Scott, Connemara after the*

Famine Journal of a Survey of the Martin Estate 1853, Dublin, 1995

Russell Lady, *Mano's Memories and Memoranda*, Bath, 1916

Shand, Alexander Innes, *Letters From the West of Ireland 1884*, Edinburgh, 1885

Semple, Maurice, Memories: *Corribwise and Otherwise*, Galway, 1999

Semple, Maurice, *Reflections on Lough Corrib*, Galway, 1973

Semple, Maurice, *By the Corribside*, Galway, 1981

Semple, Maurice, *Where the River Corrib Flows*, 1988

Smith, Harry Worcester, A *Sporting Tour Through Ireland England Wales and France in the years 1912–13*, Vol.1, Columbia, South Carolina, 1925.

Spellissy, Sean, *The History of Galway*, Limerick, 1999

Vaughan, W. E., *Landlords and Tenants in Ireland 1848-1904*, Dundalk, 1984

Vaughan, W. E., *Landlords and Tenants in Mid-Victorian Ireland*, Oxford, 1994

Vaughan, W. E., *Sin, Sheep and Scotsmen* John George Adair and the Derryveagh Evictions 1861, Belfast, 1983

Villiers-Tuthill, Katherine, *Patient Endurance, The Great Famine in Connemara*, Dublin, 1997

Wakeman, W. F., *The Tourists Guide to Ireland*, Dublin, c.1885

Webster, W. B., *Ireland Considered as a Field for Investment or Residence*, London, 1853

Williams, Jeremy, *A Companion Guide to Architecture in Ireland 1837-1921*, Dublin, 1994

The Collected Poems of W.B. Yeats, London, 1955

Young, Filson, *Ireland at the Cross Roads*, London, 1903

Miscellaneous

Album of Newspaper Cuttings of the Prince of Wales' visit to Ashford Castle in 1905 in the possession of the Hon. Garech Browne; Marriage, obituaries, funeral notices, the Royal visit, appreciations of Lord and Lady Ardilaun in the Dublin, Cork, Kerry, and Galway Newspapers, also articles on rent reduction, tenants' parties, and other newspaper material in *The Irish Times, Dublin Evening Mail, Galway Express, Tuam Herald, Skibbereen Eagle, Ballinrobe Chronicle, Killarney Echo, Kingstown and Bray Observer*, the *Cork Constitution, Cork Daily Herald, Cork Examiner, Dublin Opinion, Illustrated London News, The Times* and *The Court Circular*, kindly supplied by Sinead McCoole and Patrick Melvin. All these copies and extracts are deposited with the Memorabilia Room at Ashford Castle; Ordinance Survey Maps of 1840.